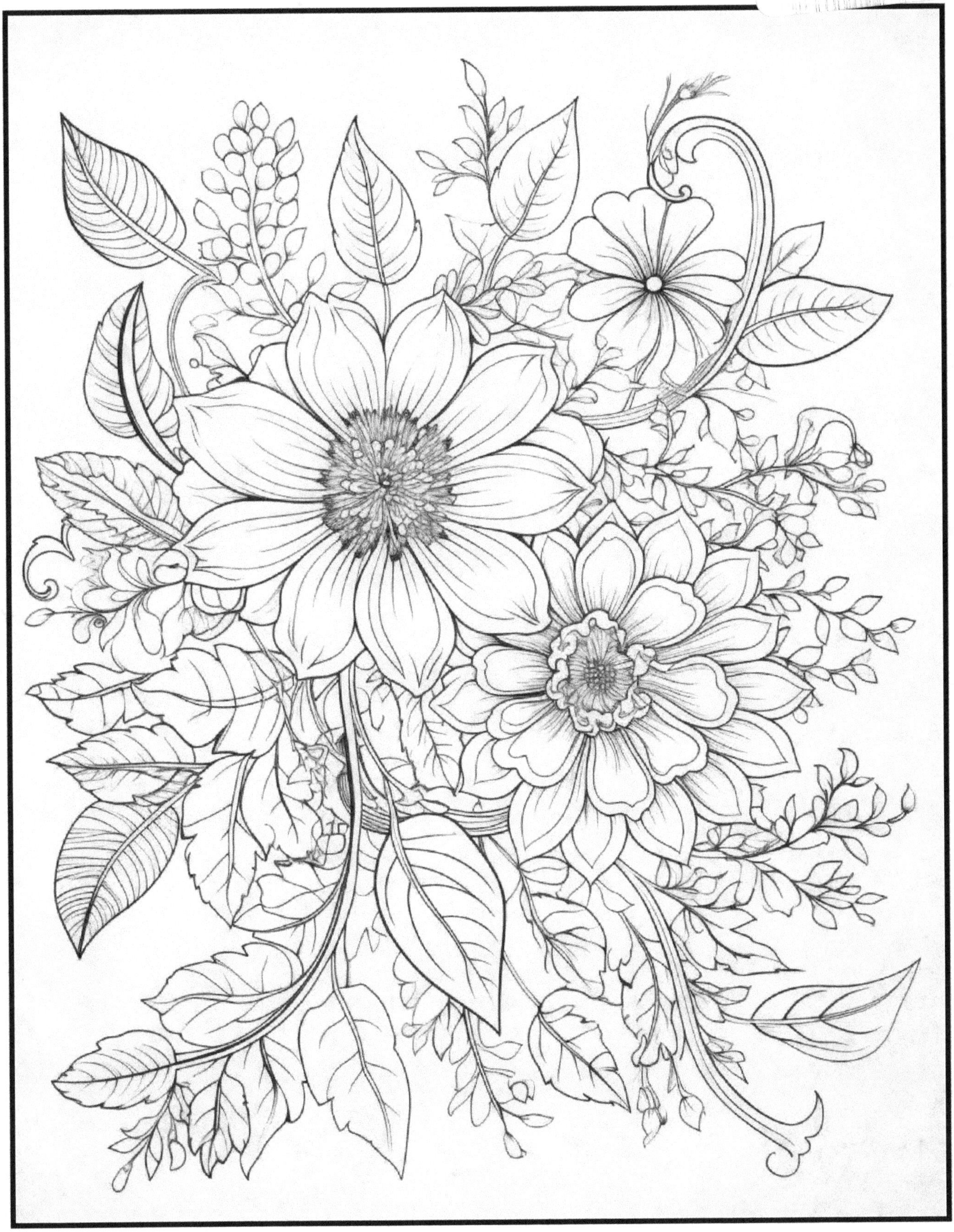

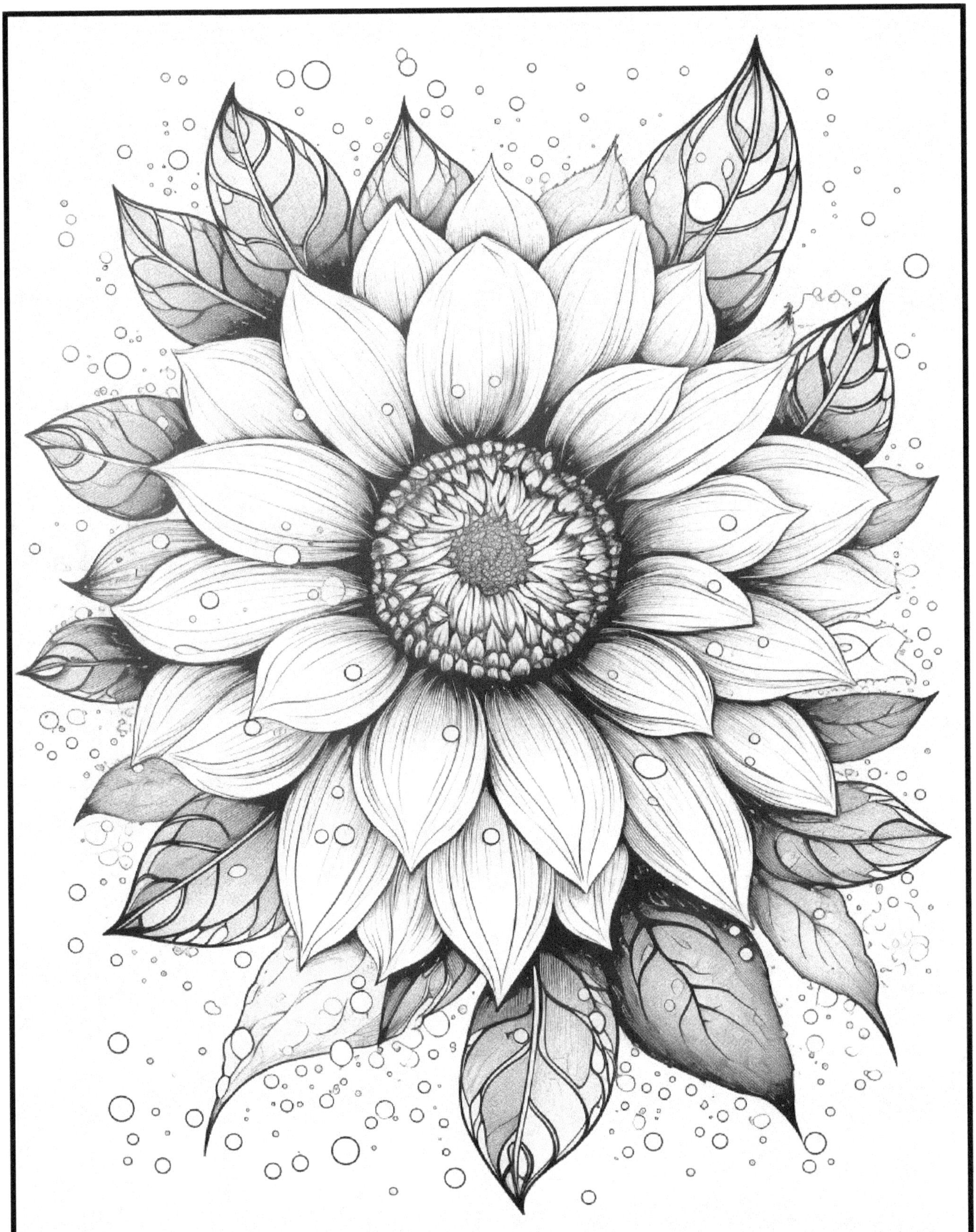

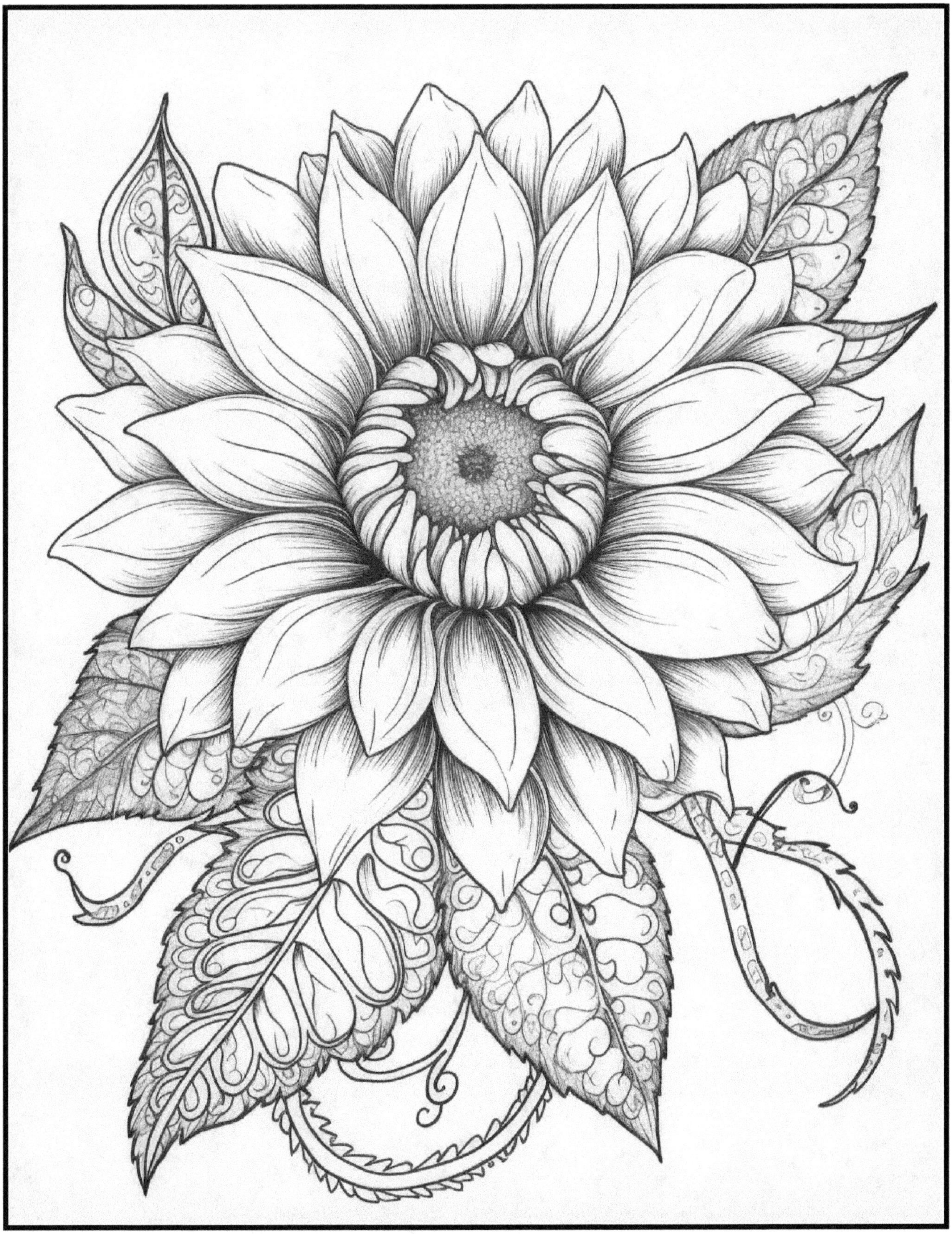

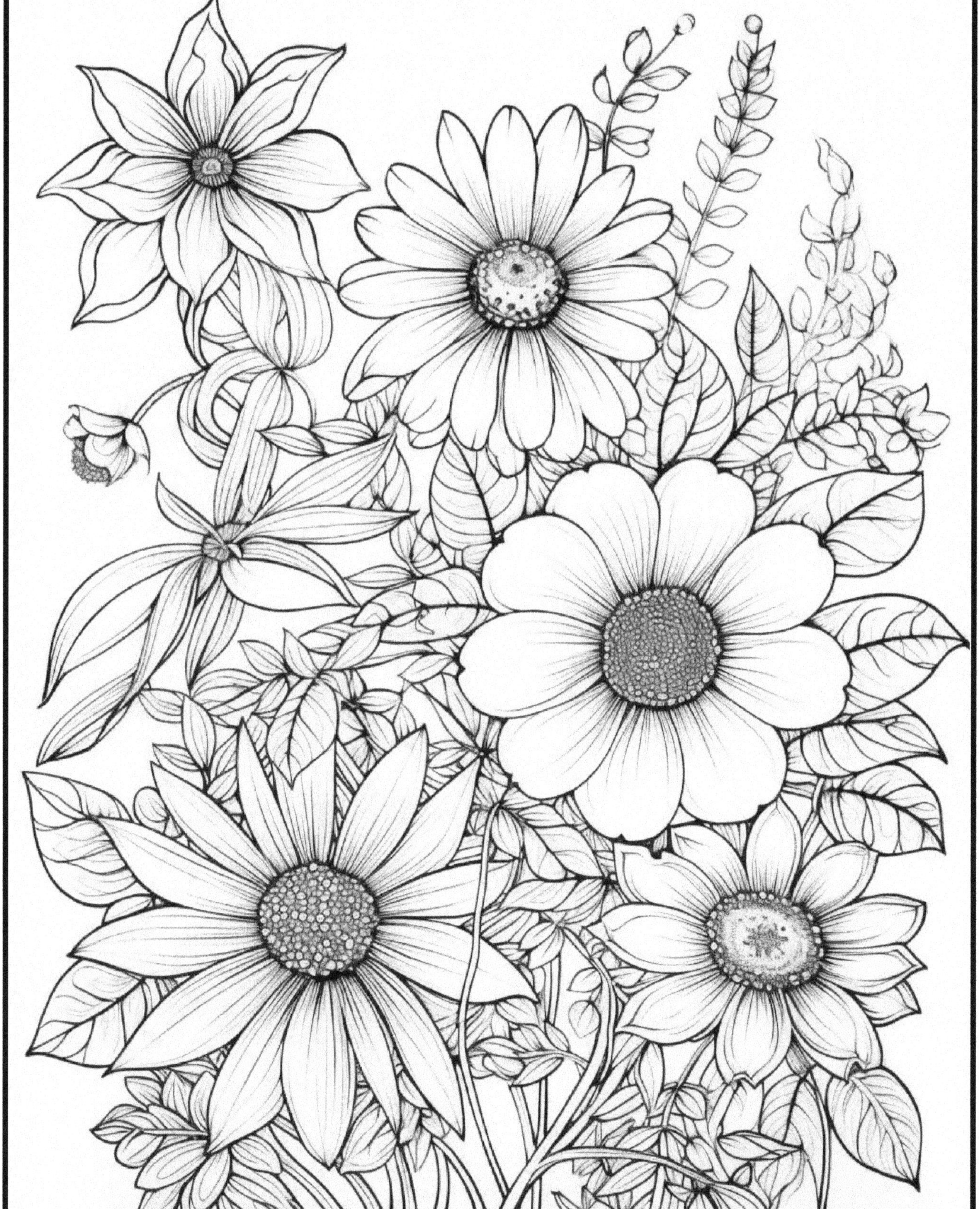

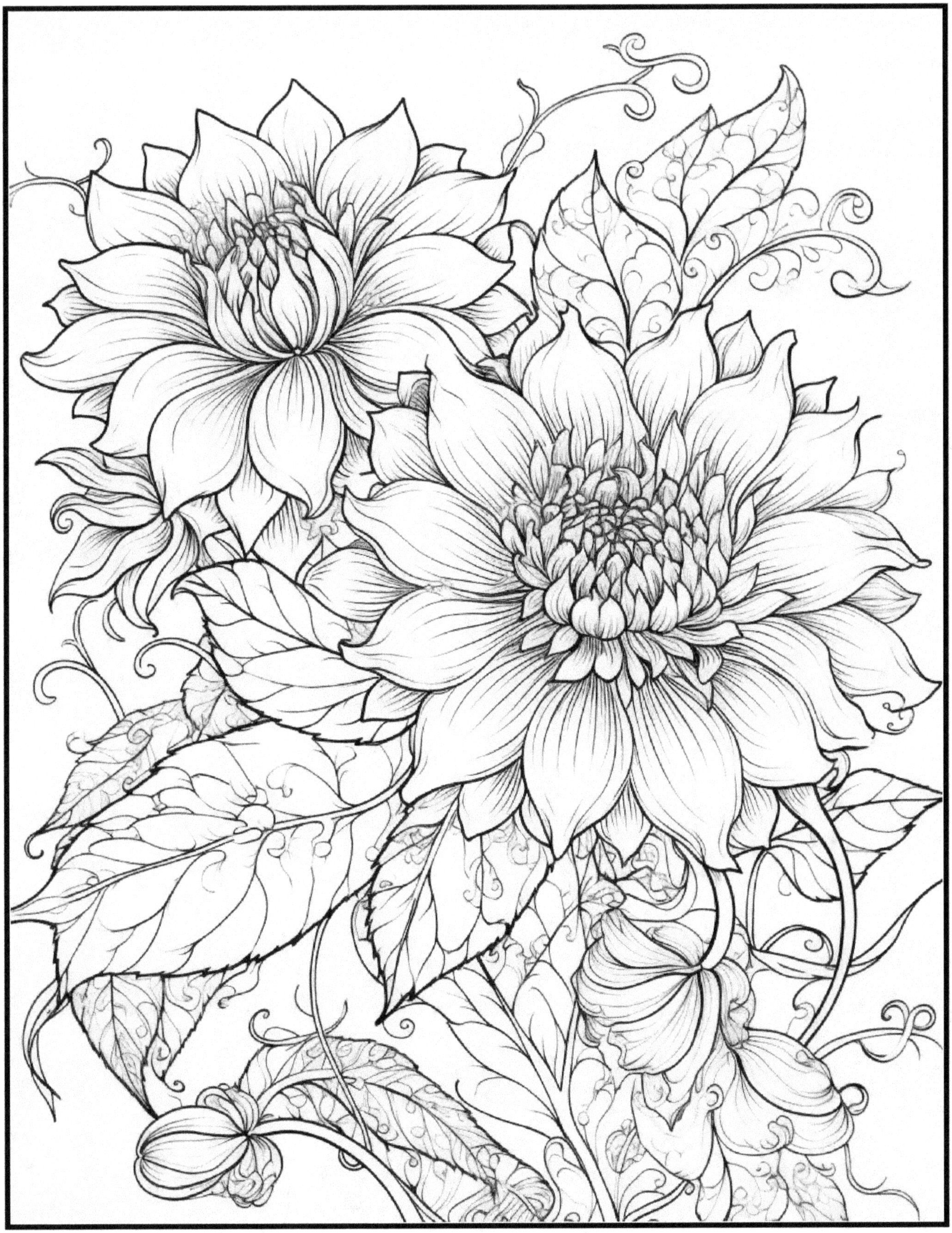

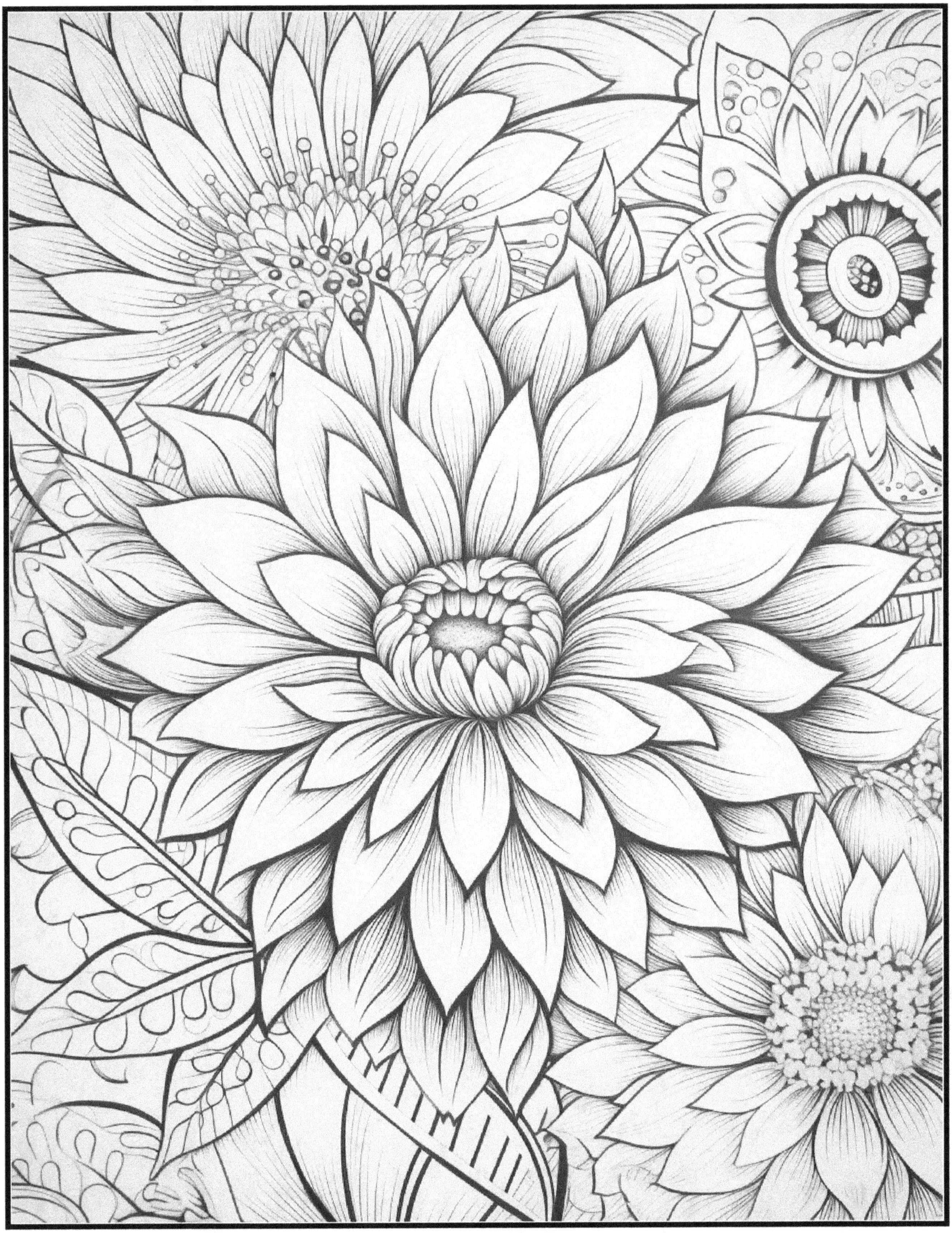

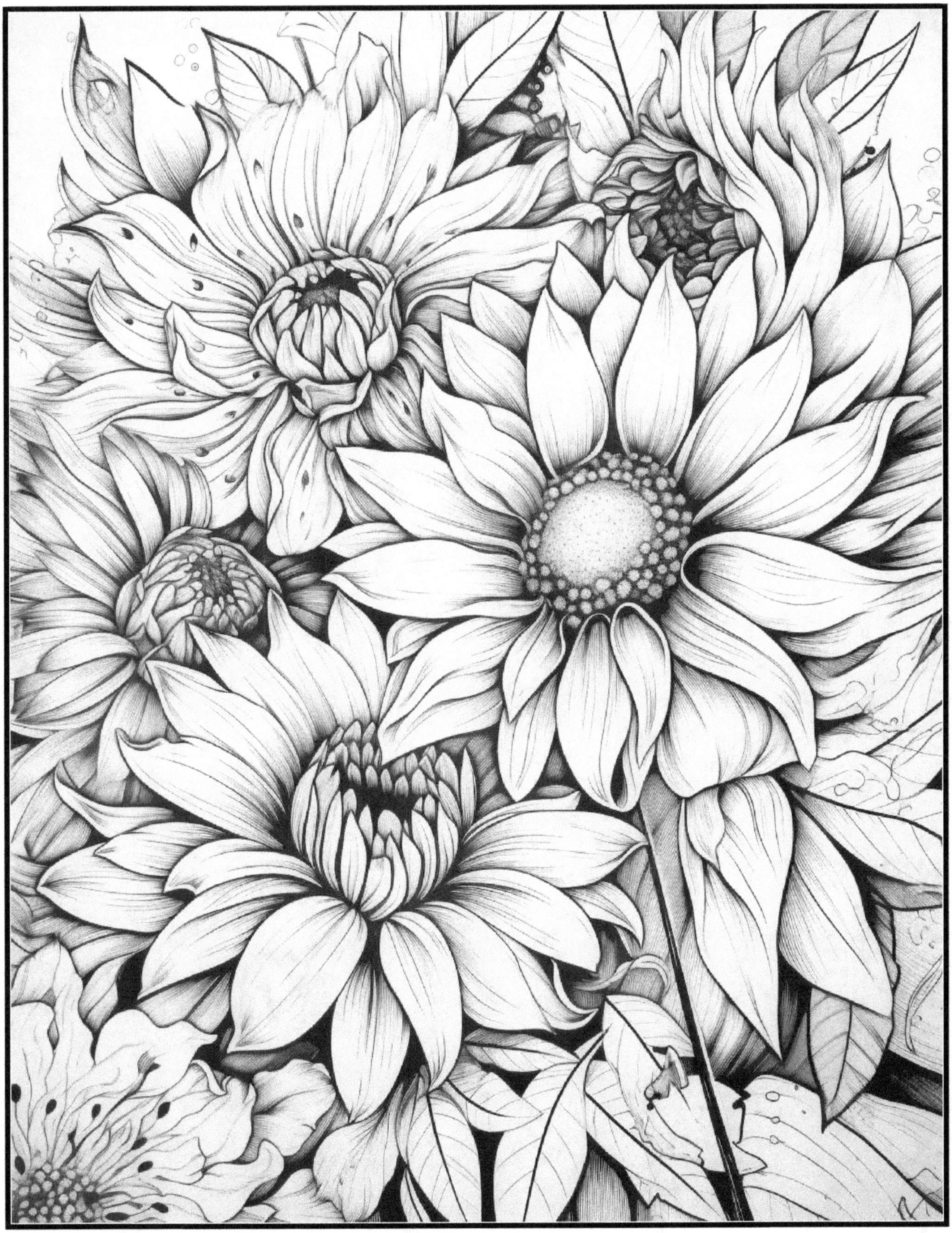

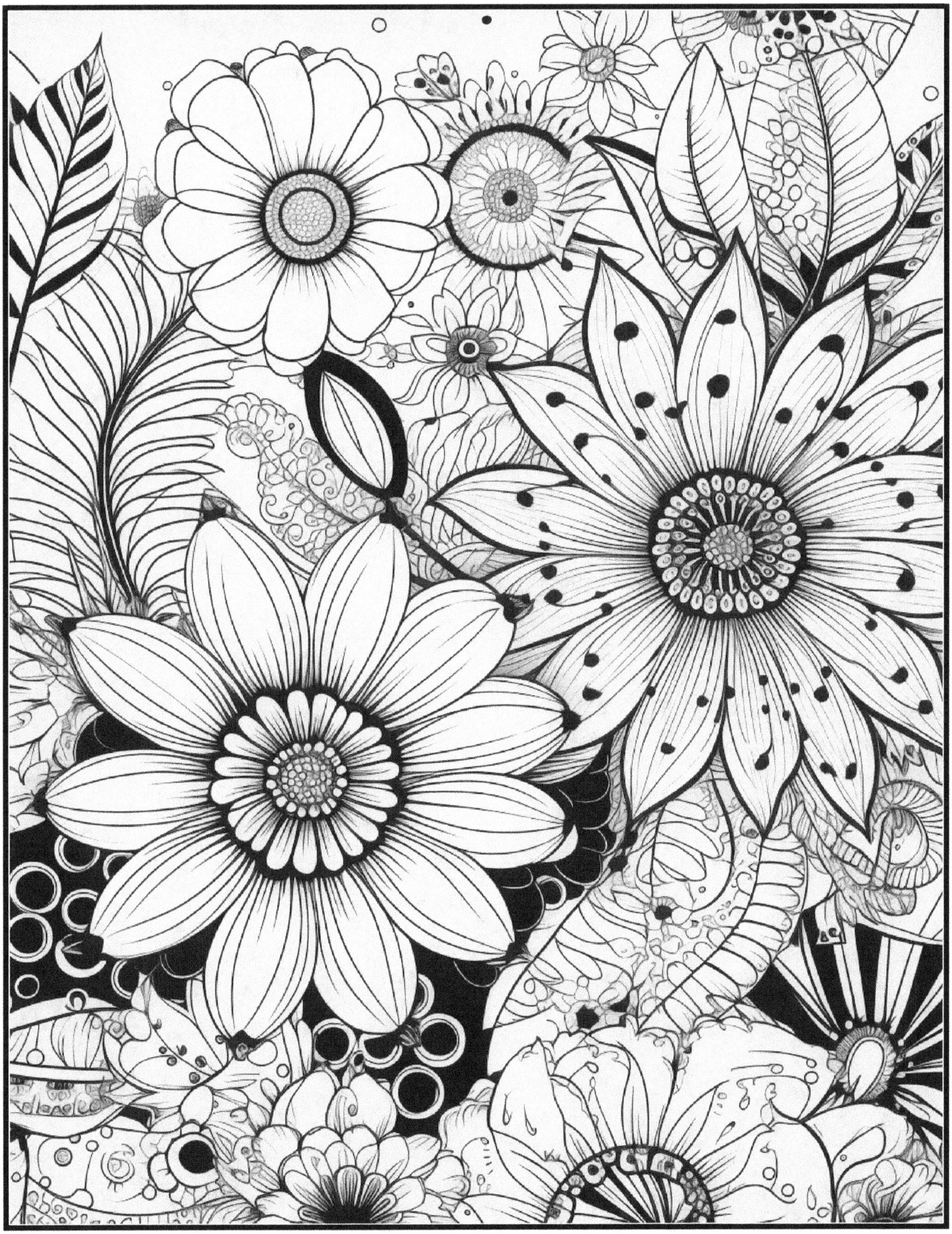

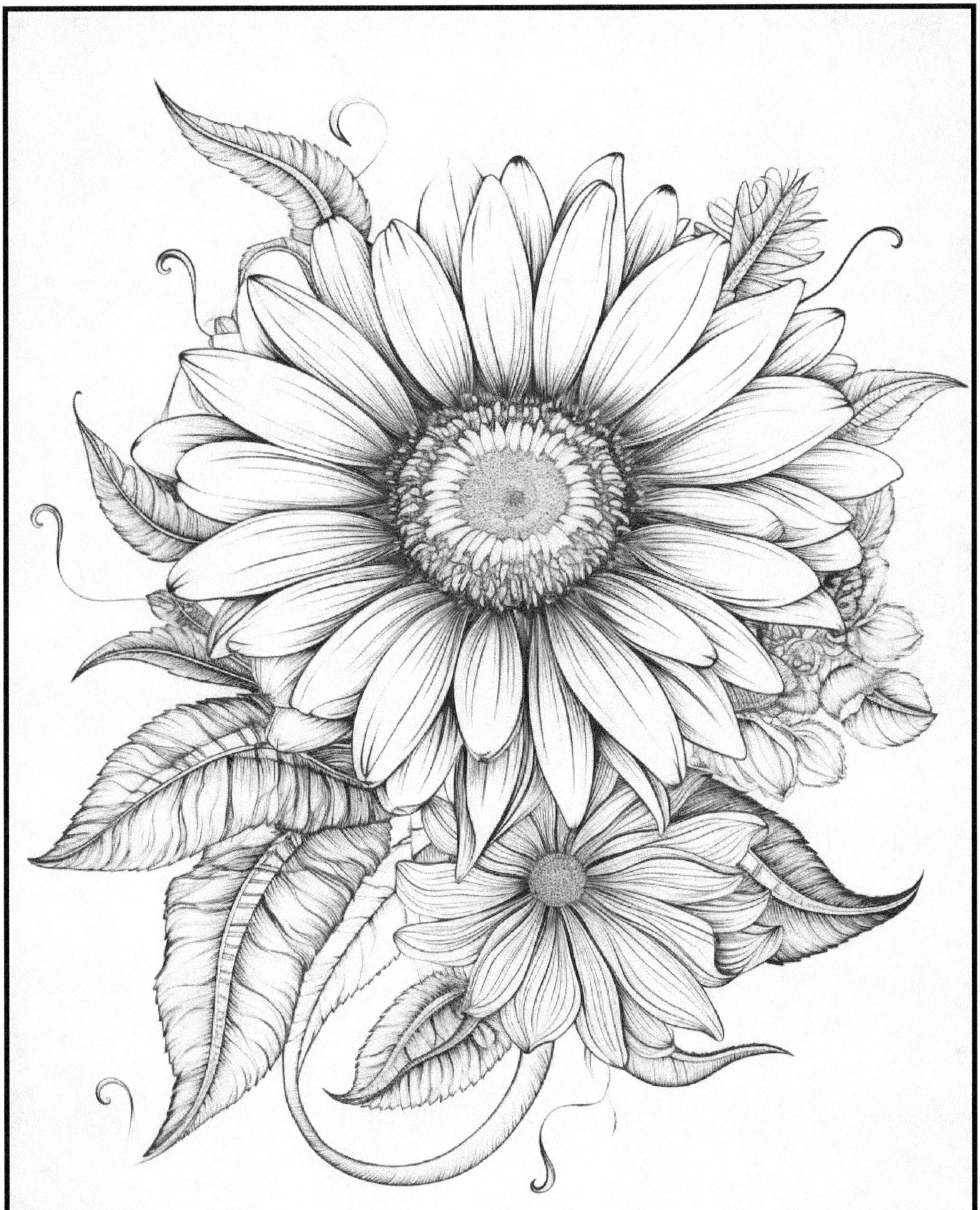

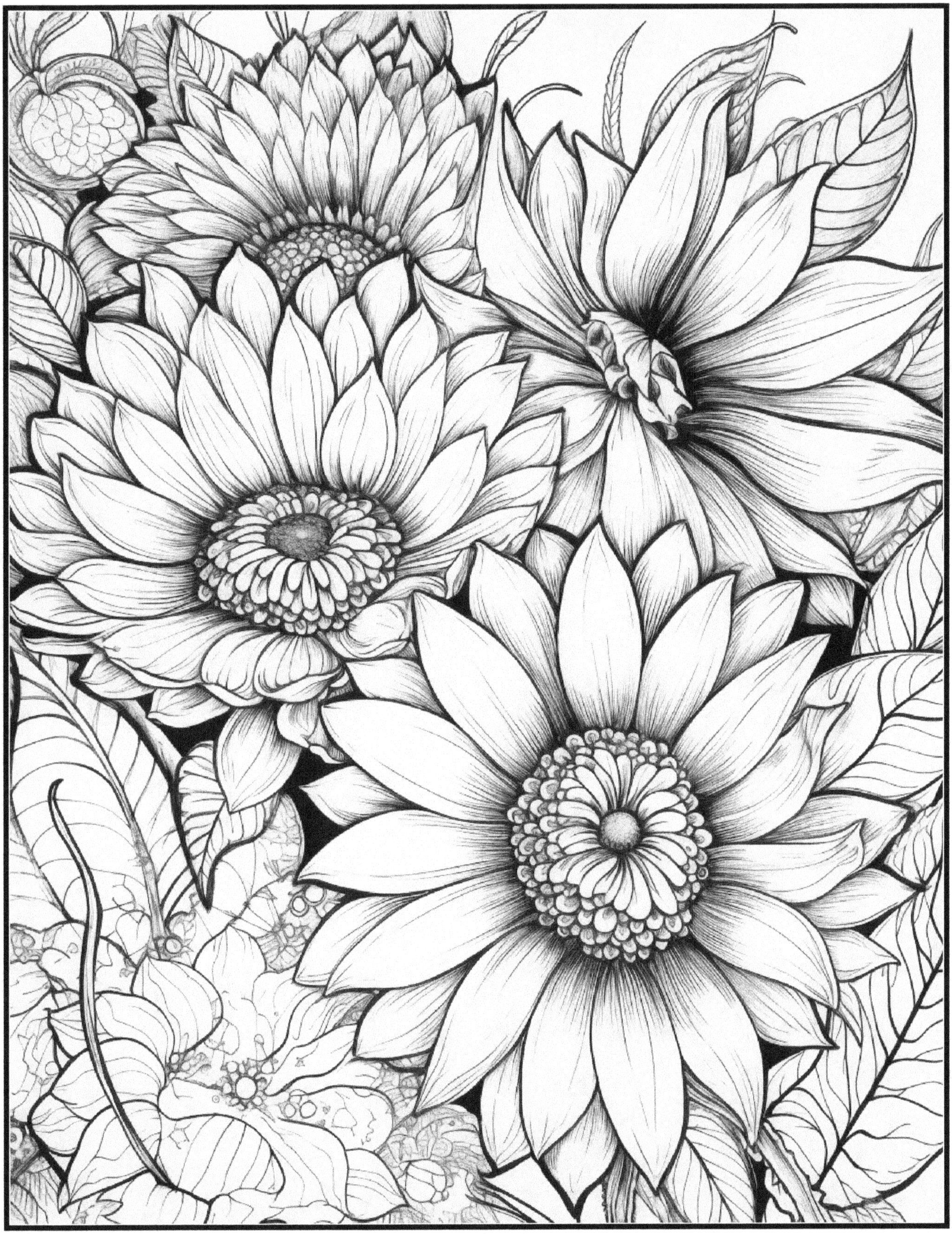

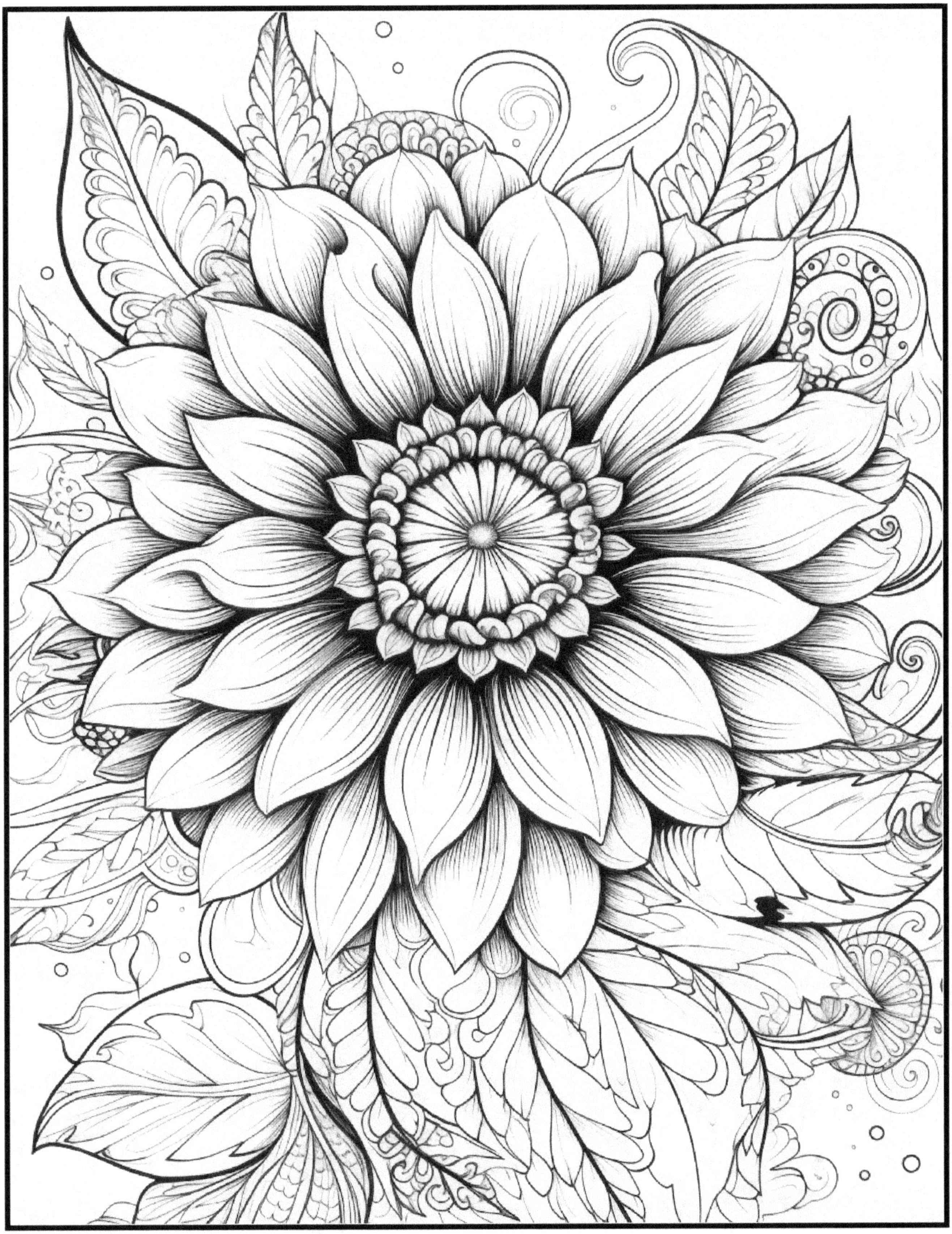

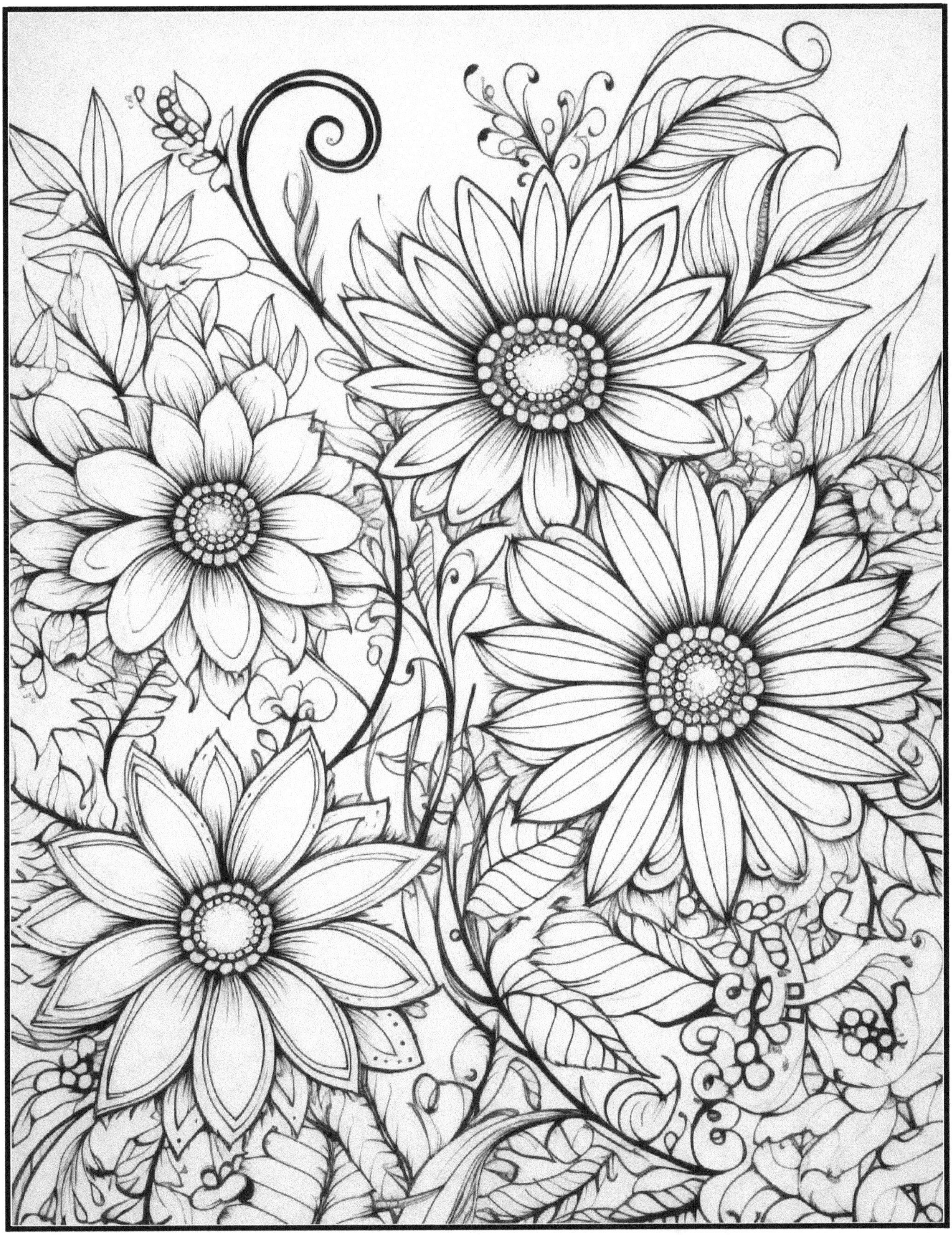

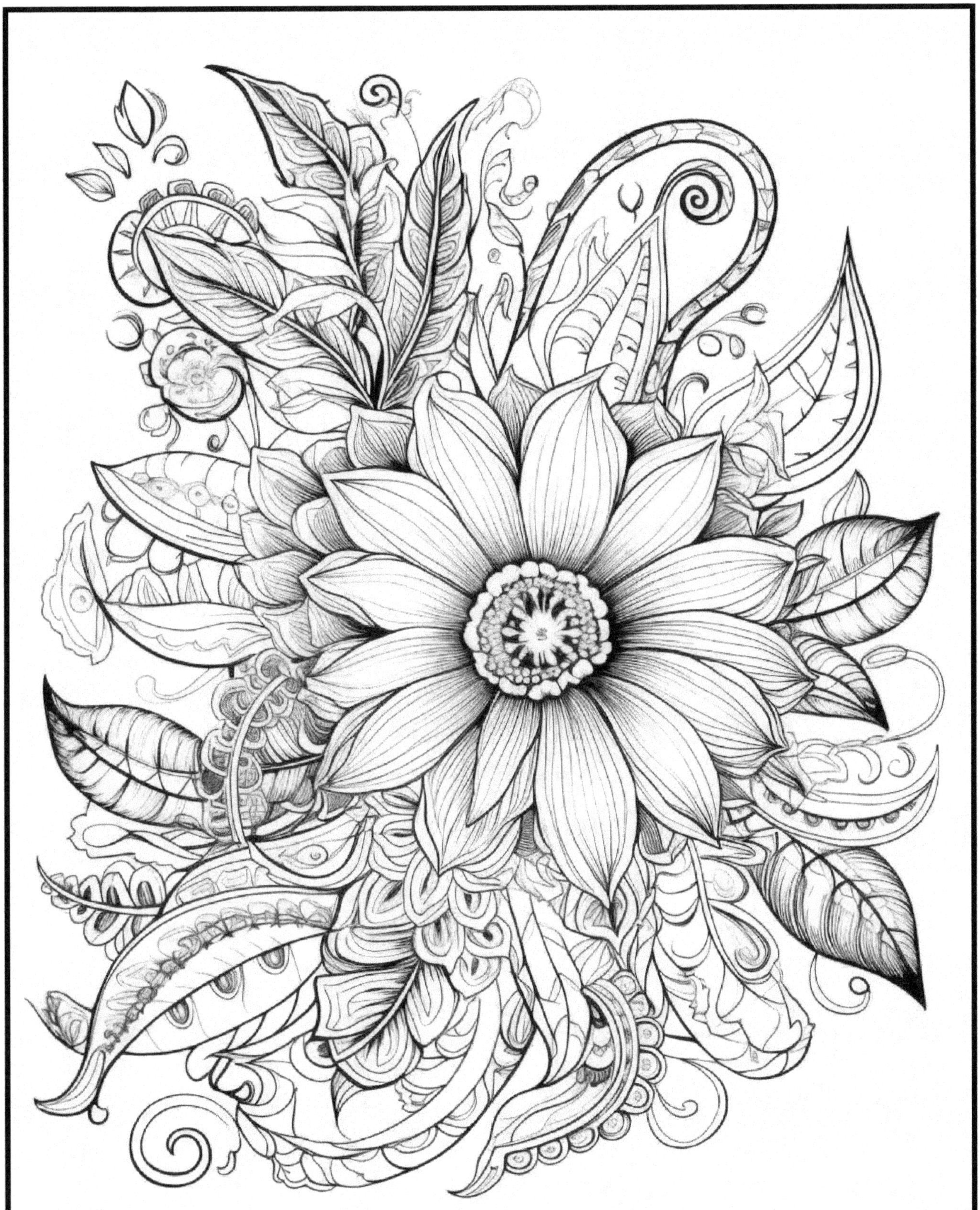

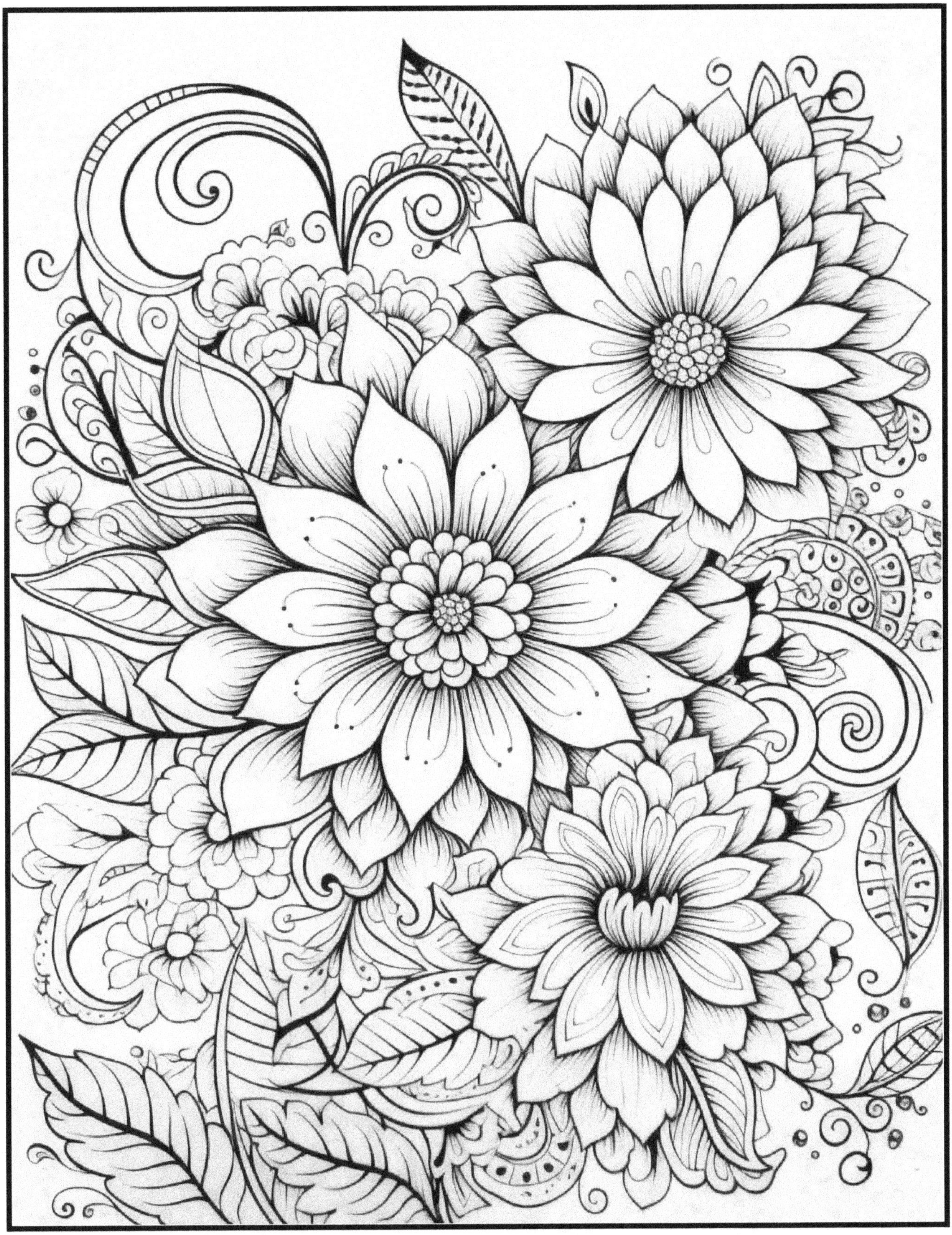

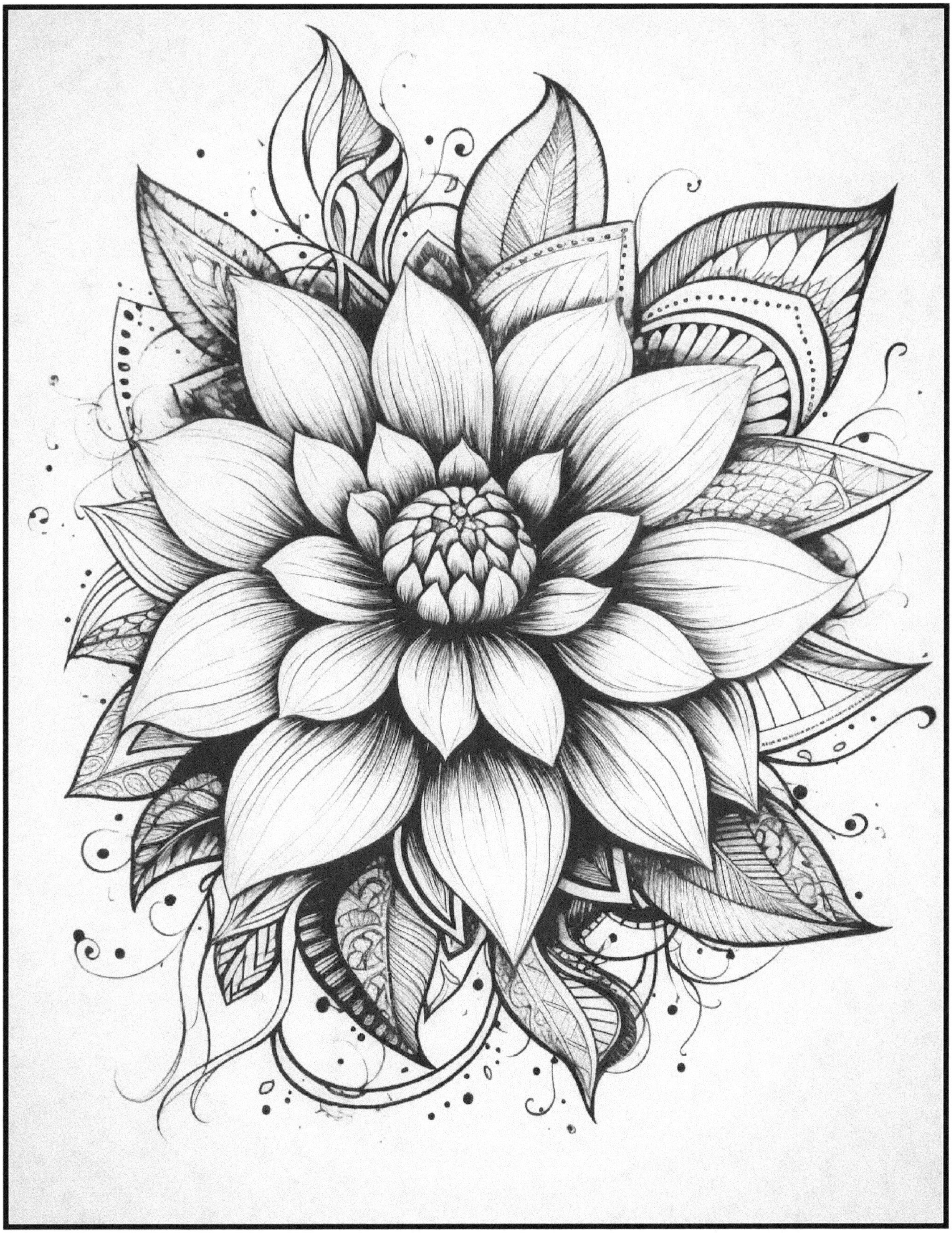

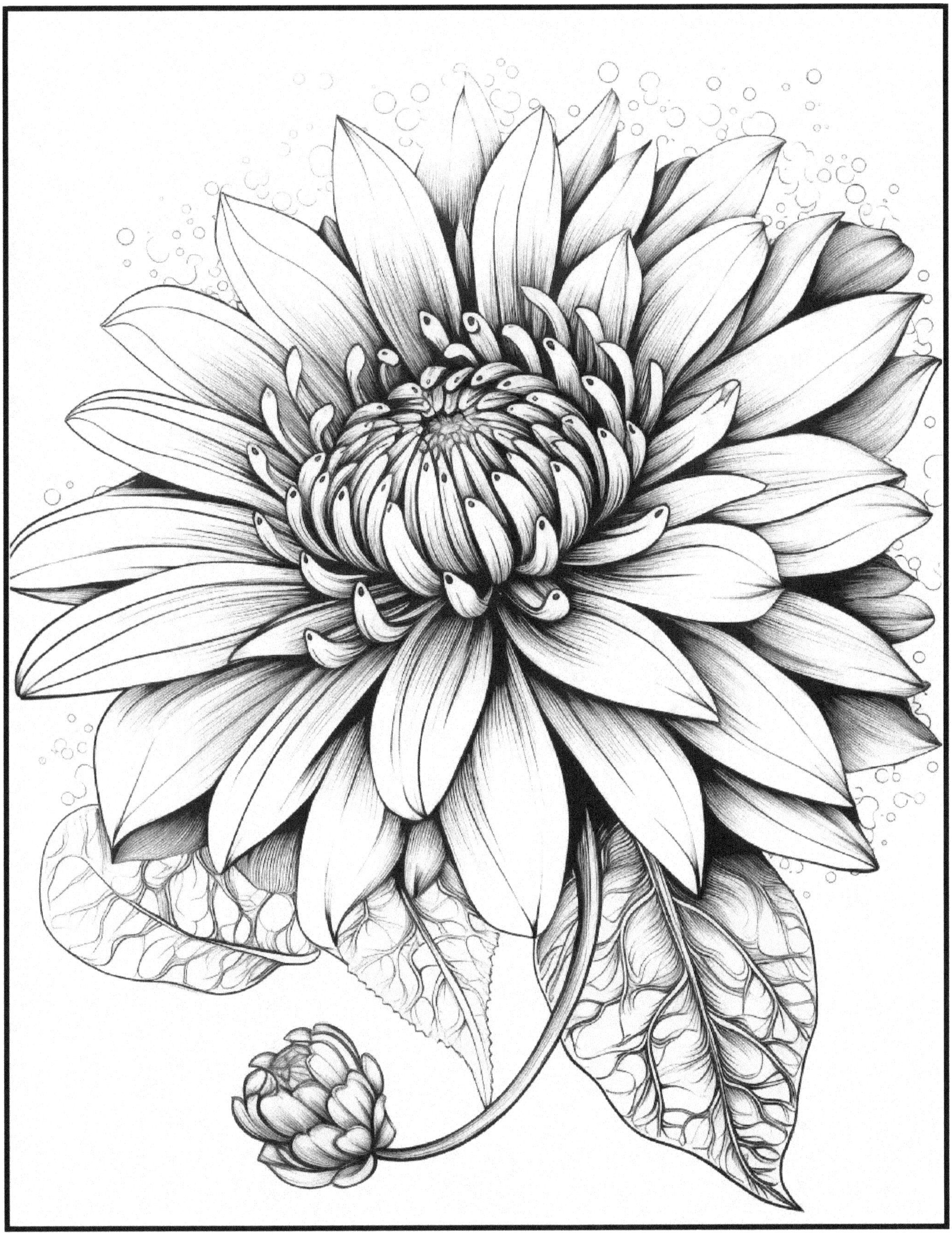

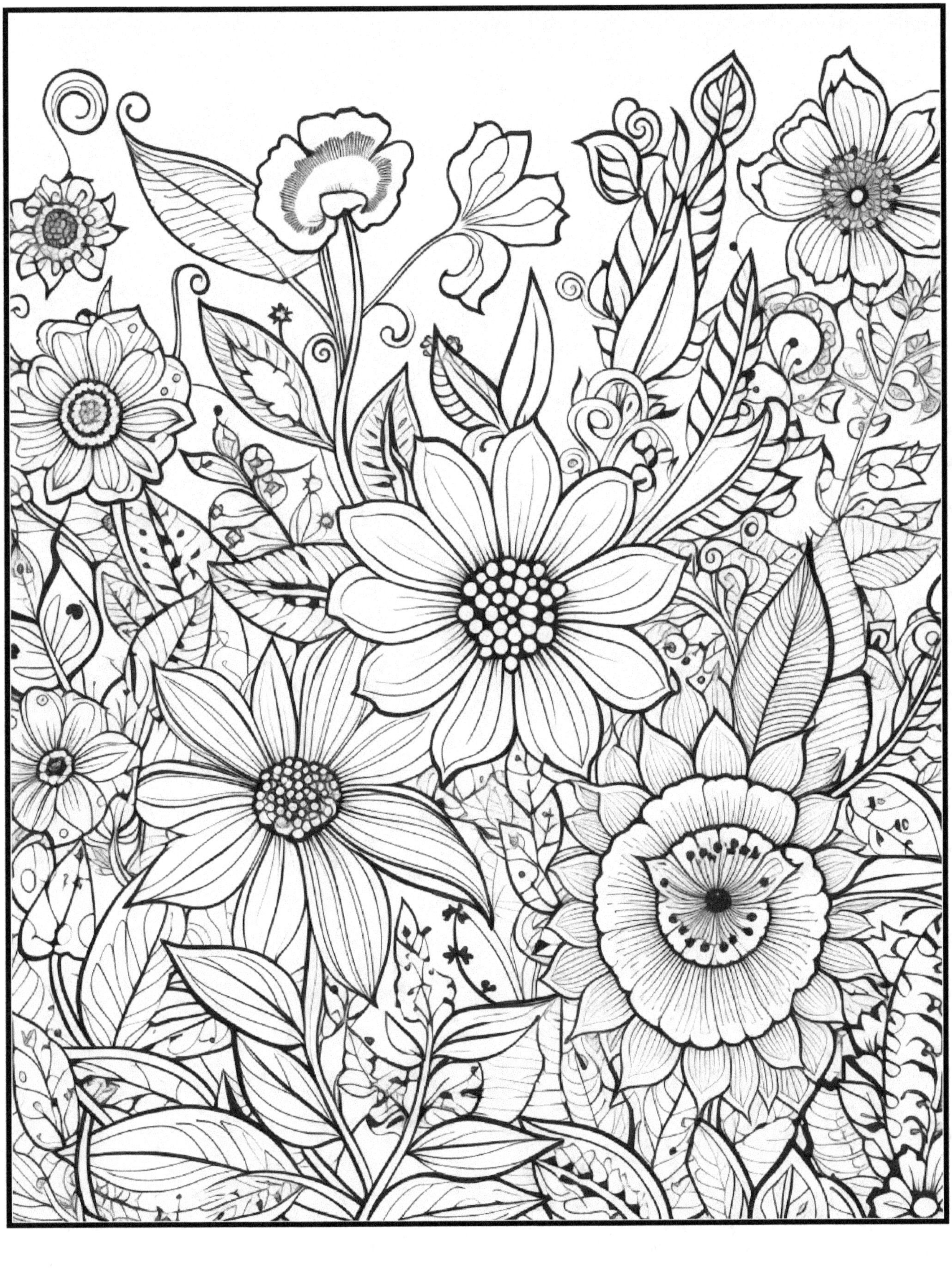

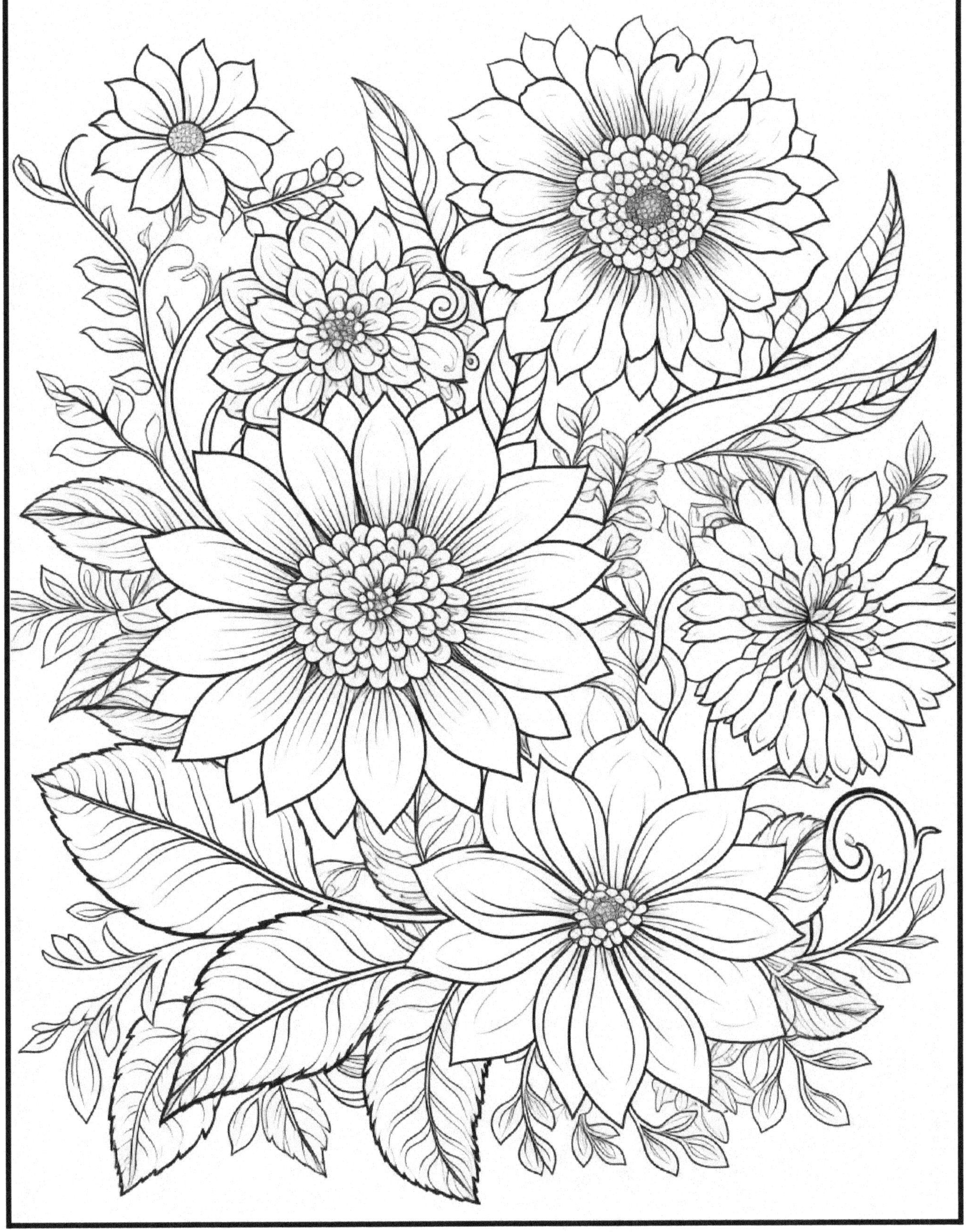

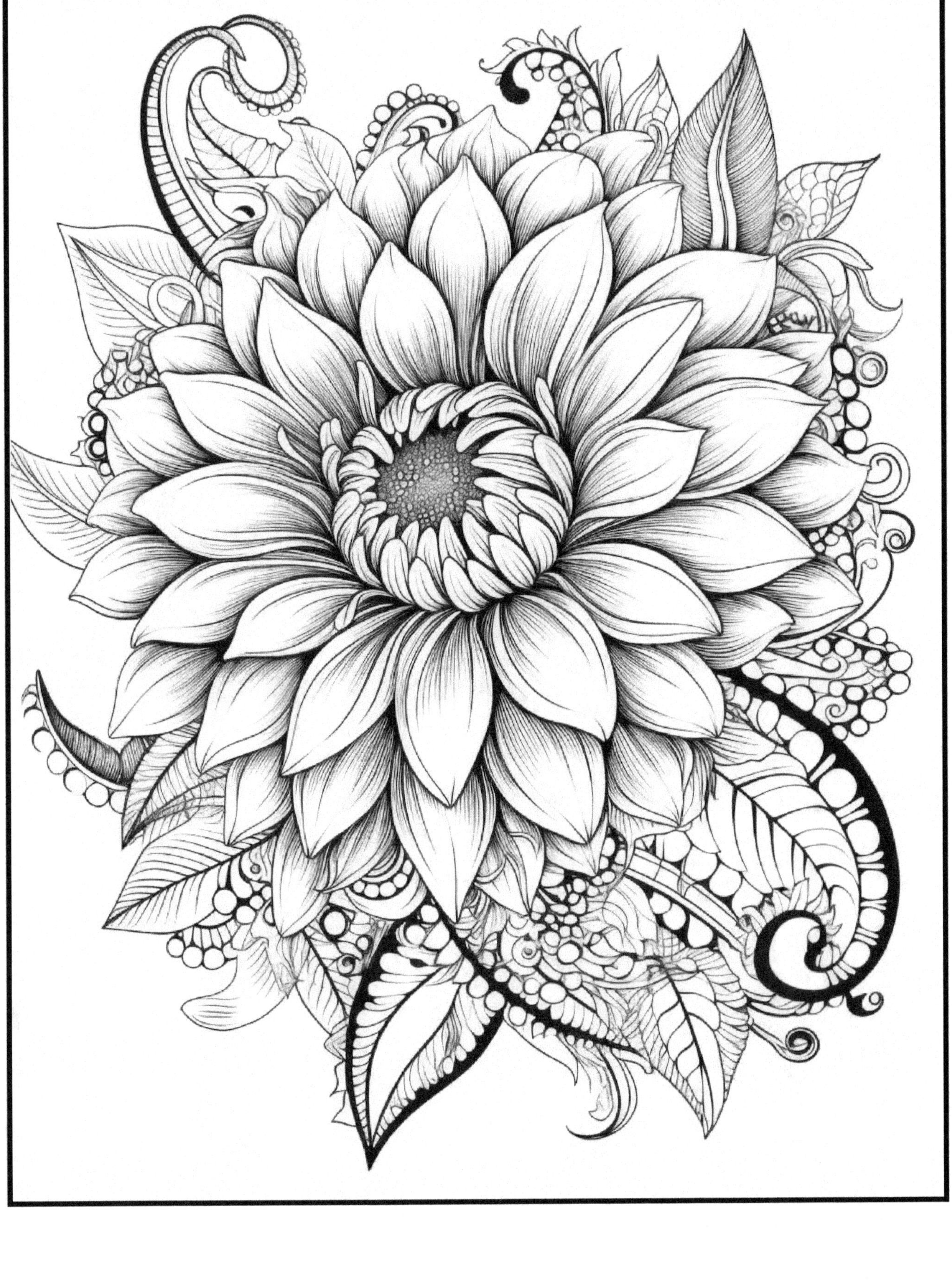

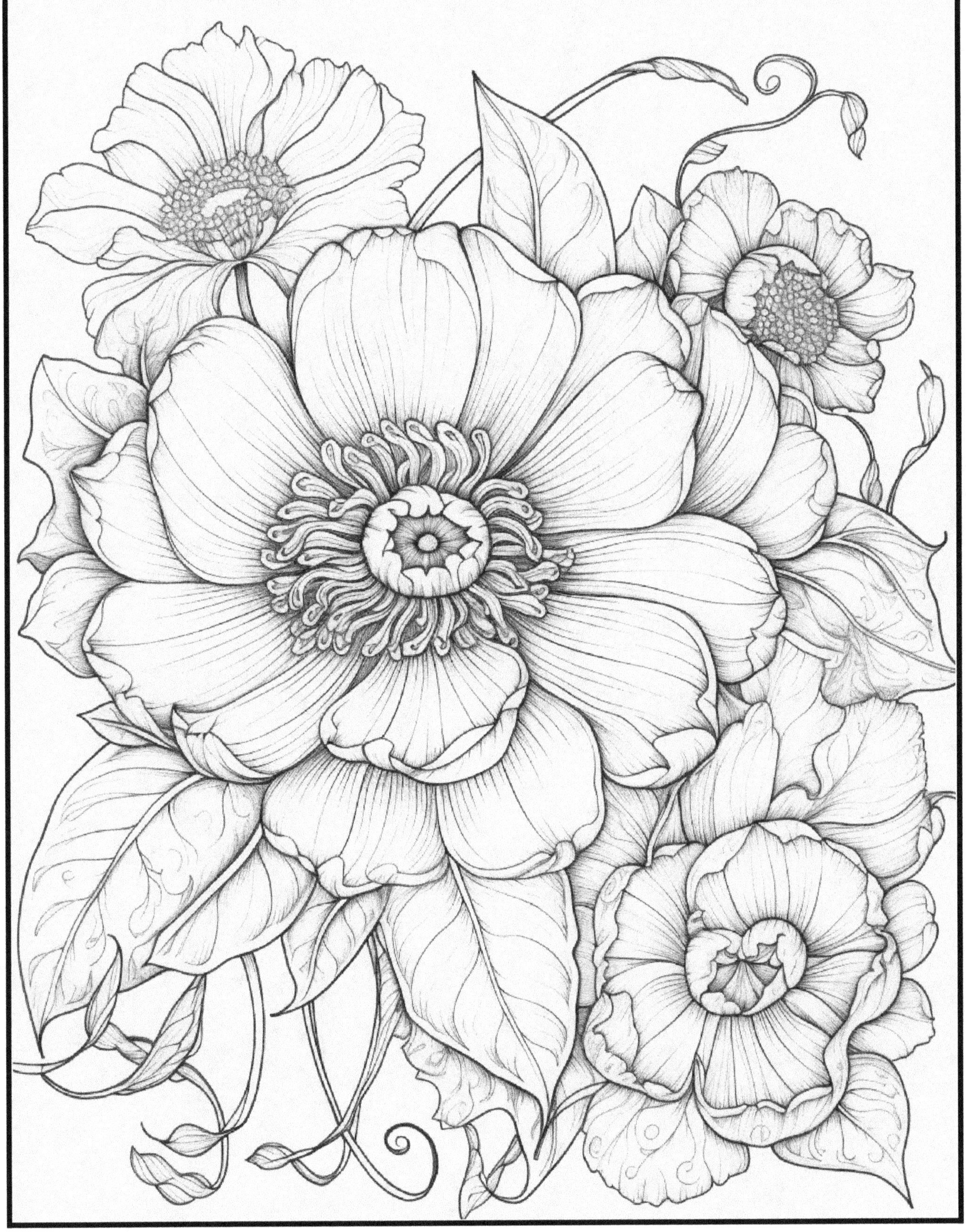

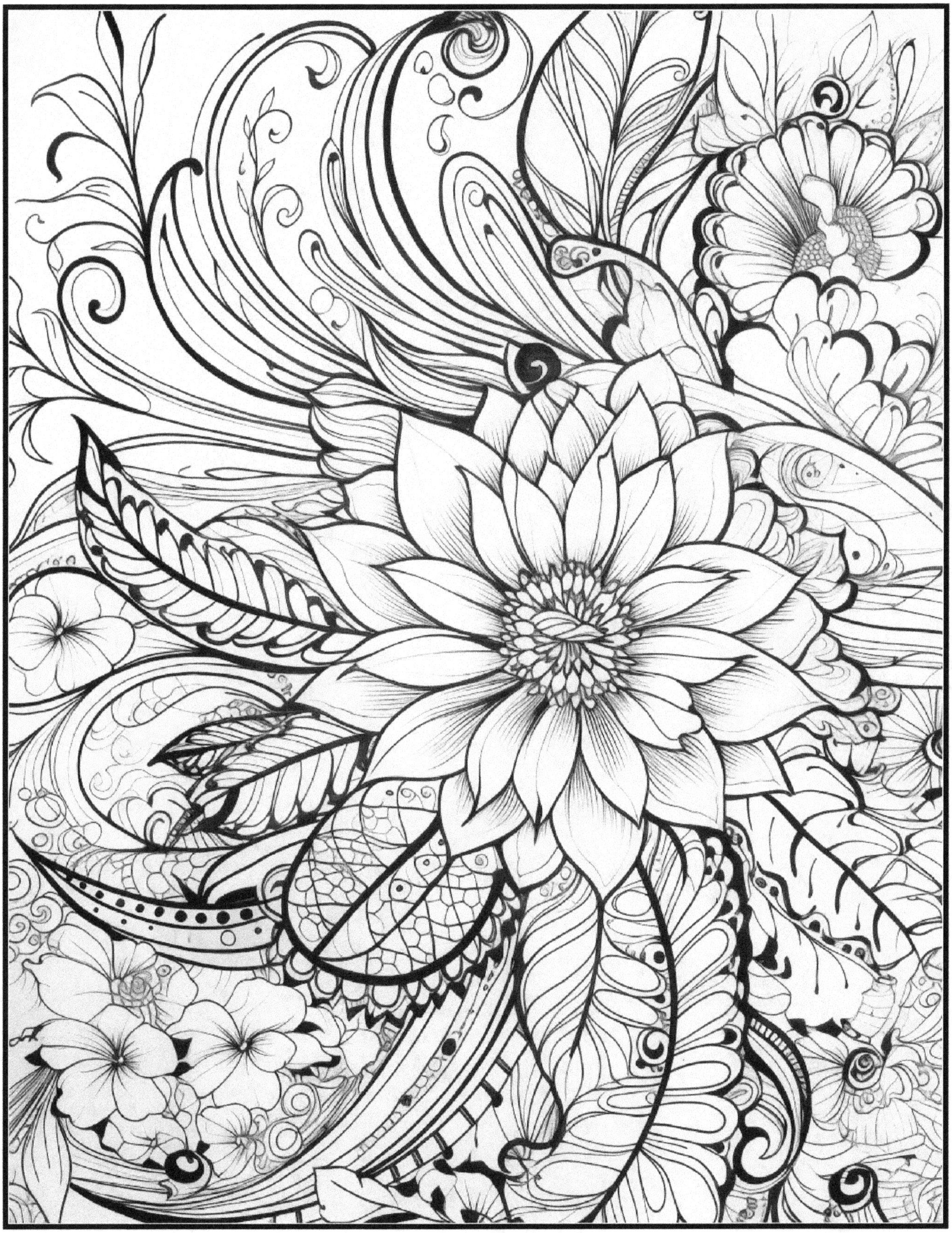

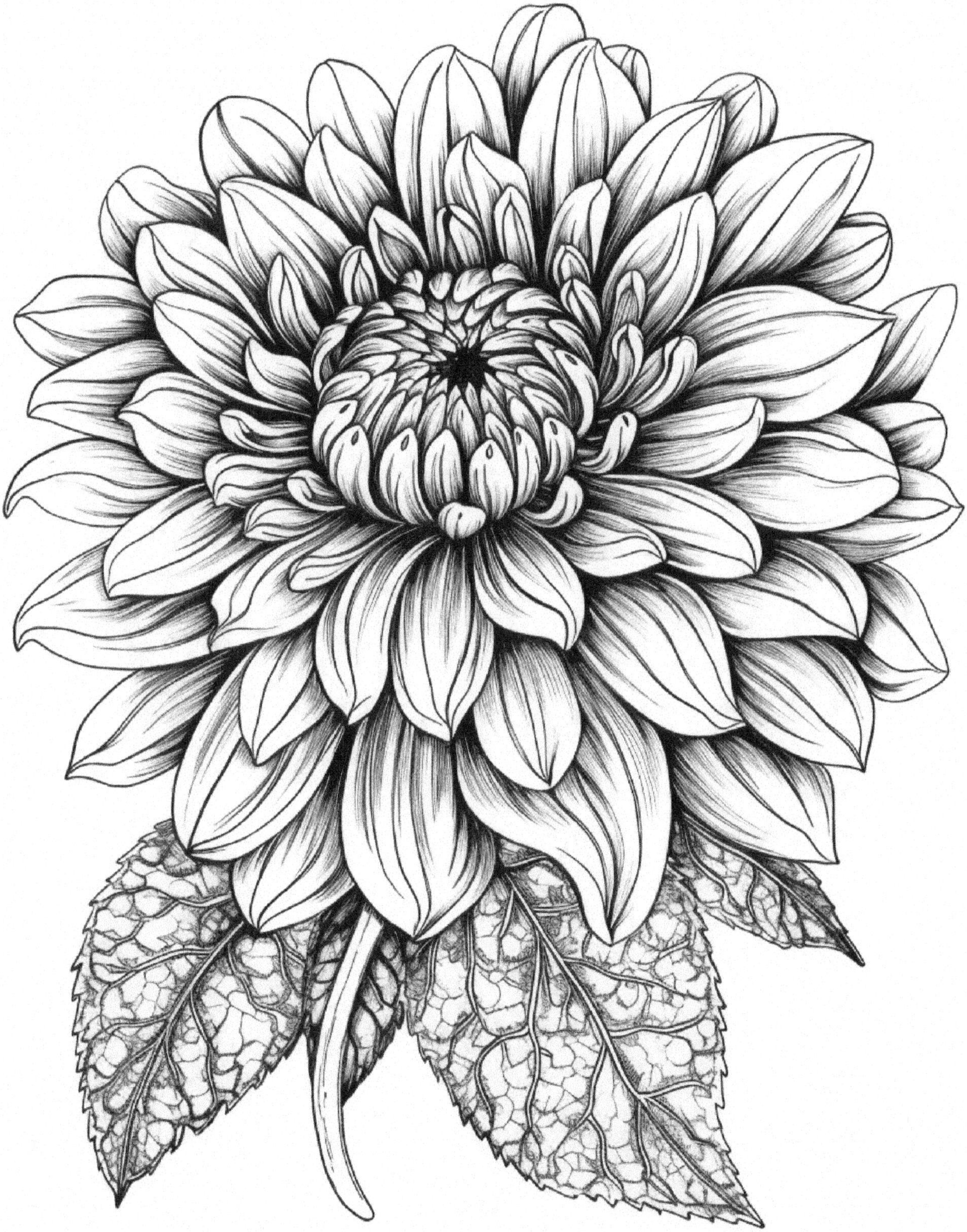

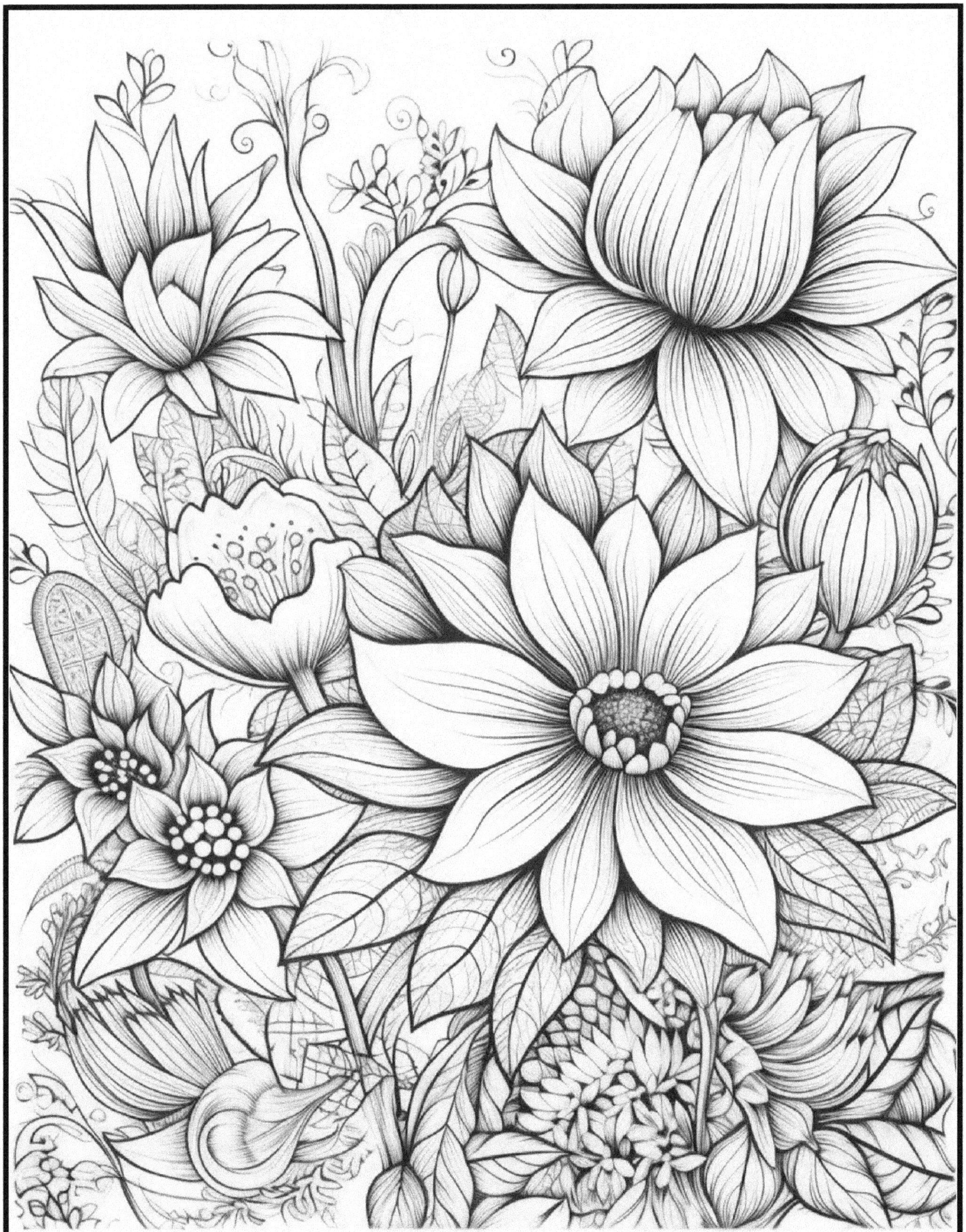

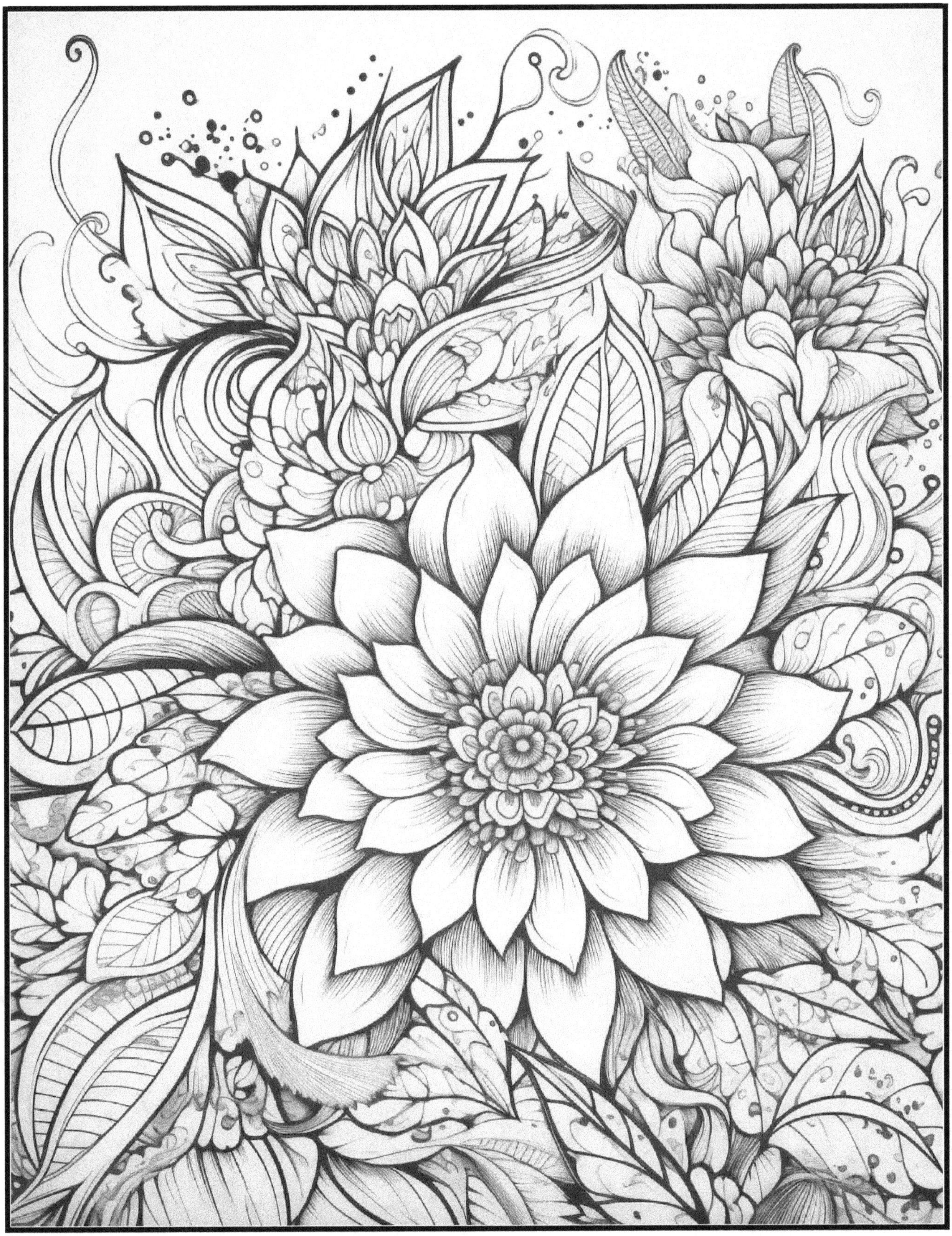

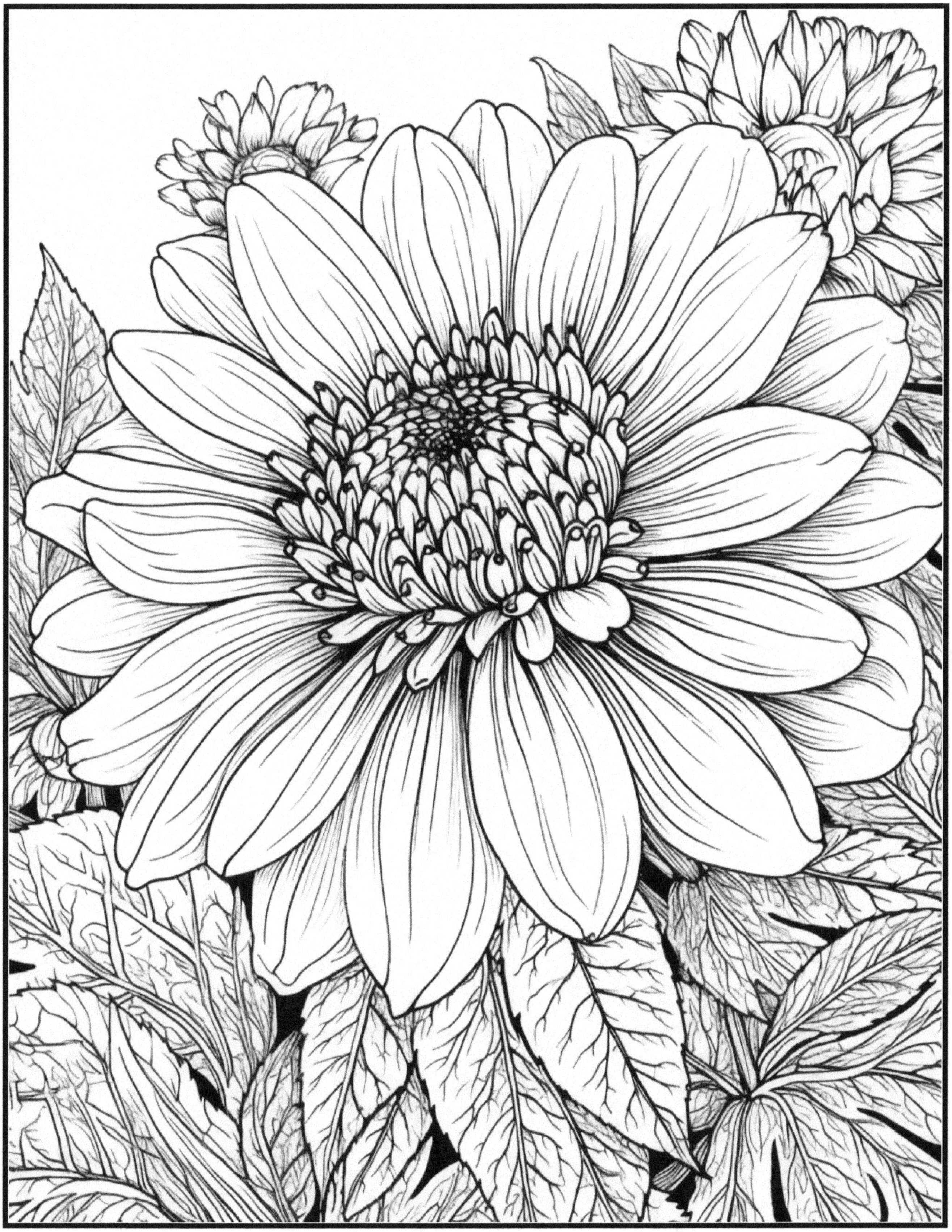

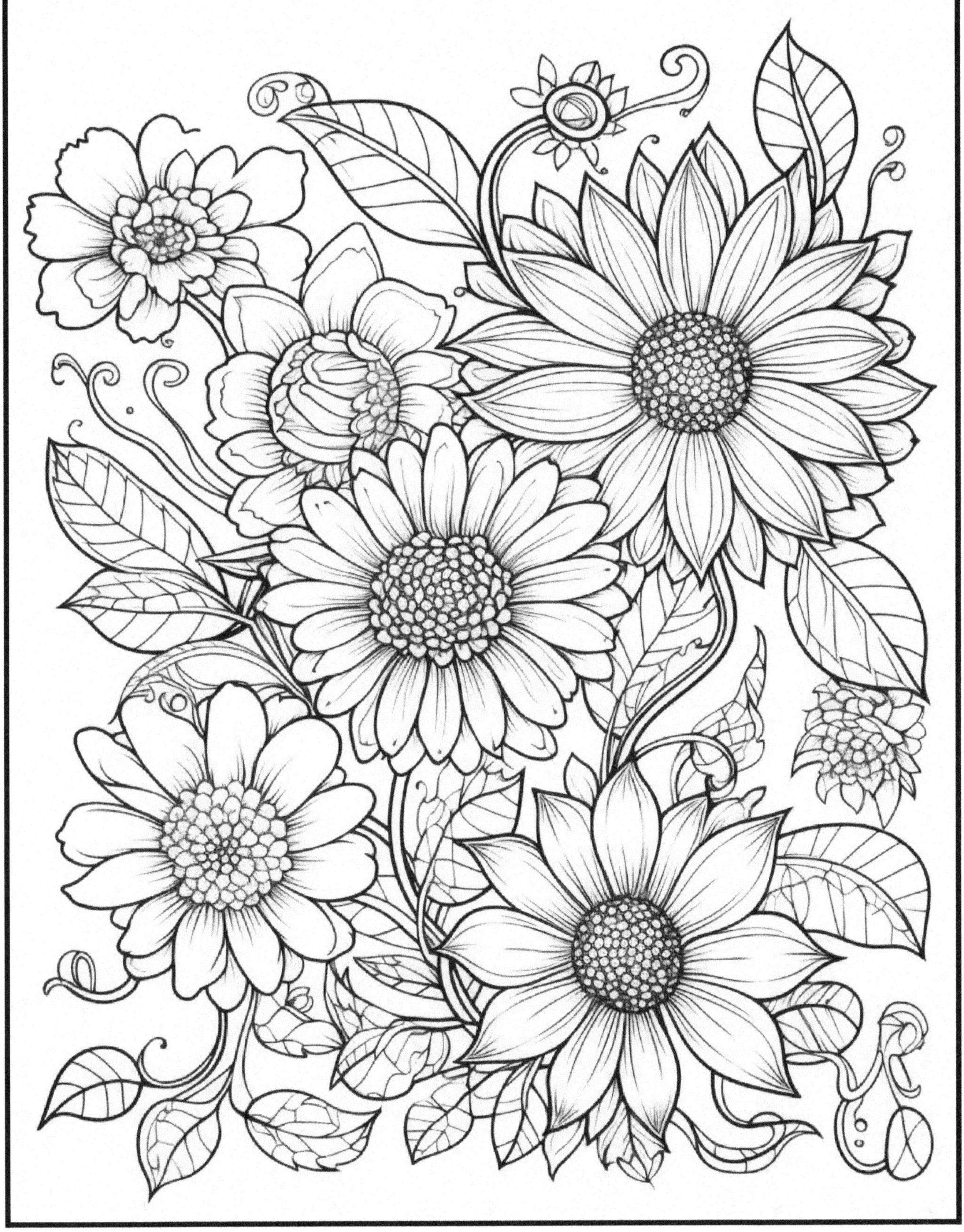

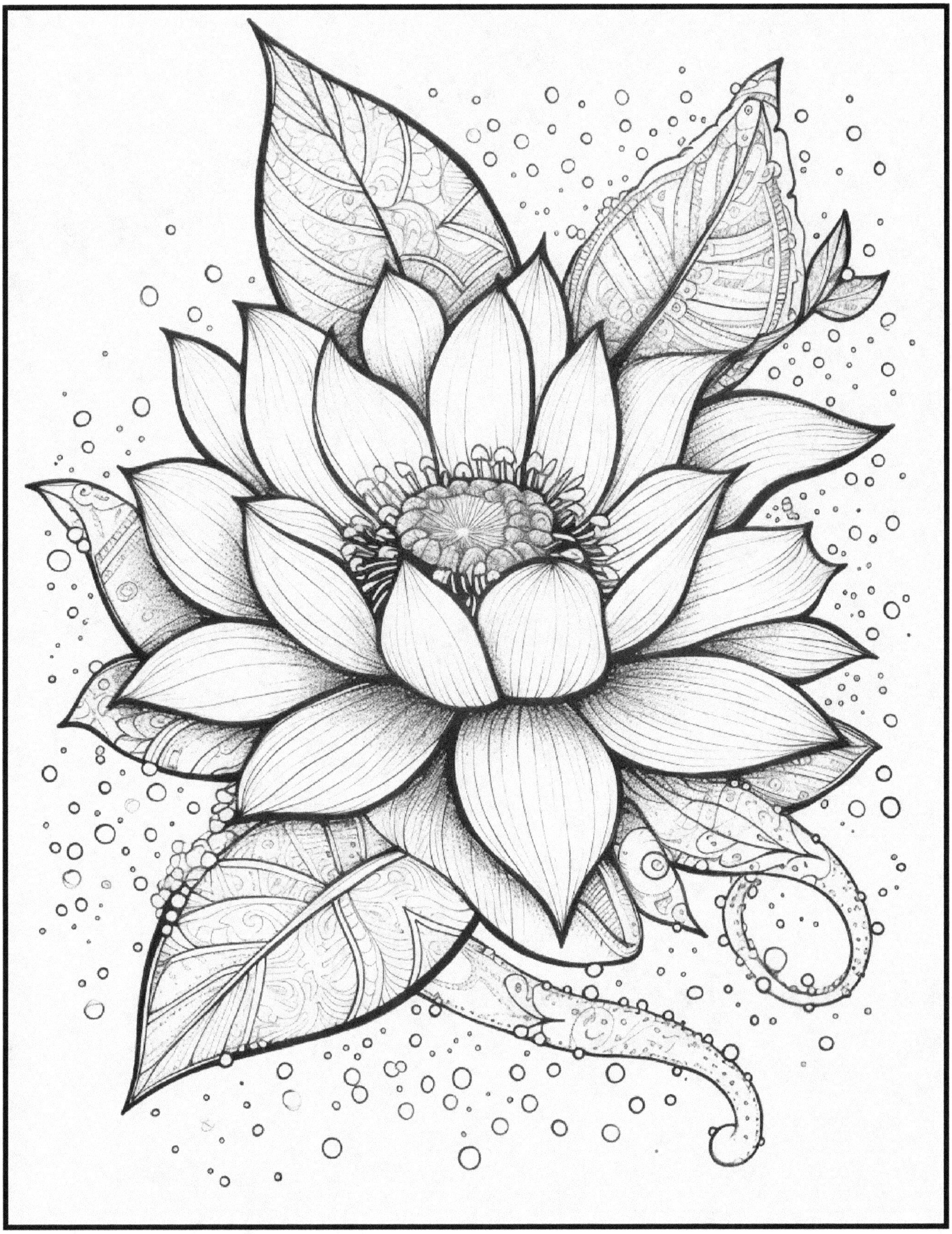

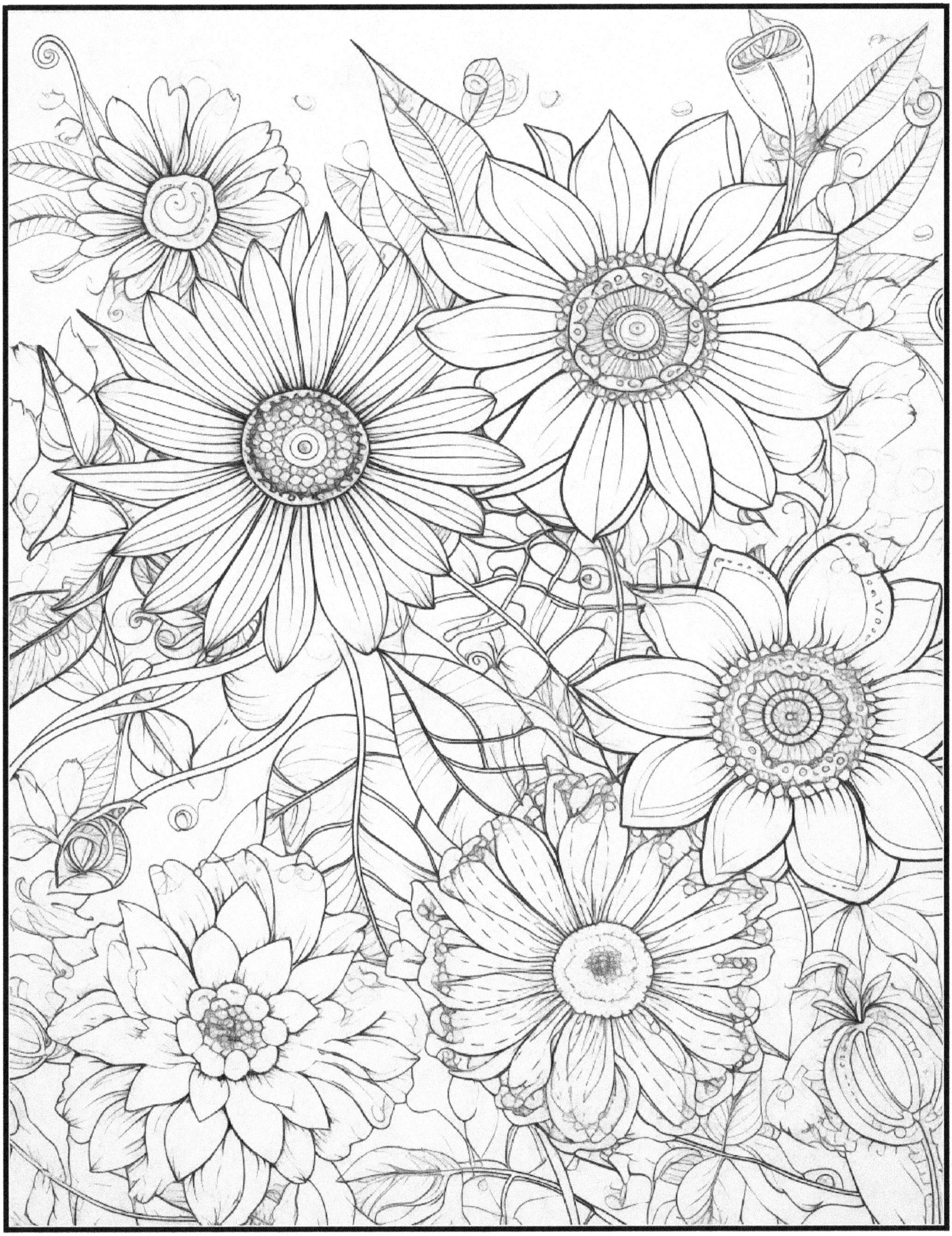

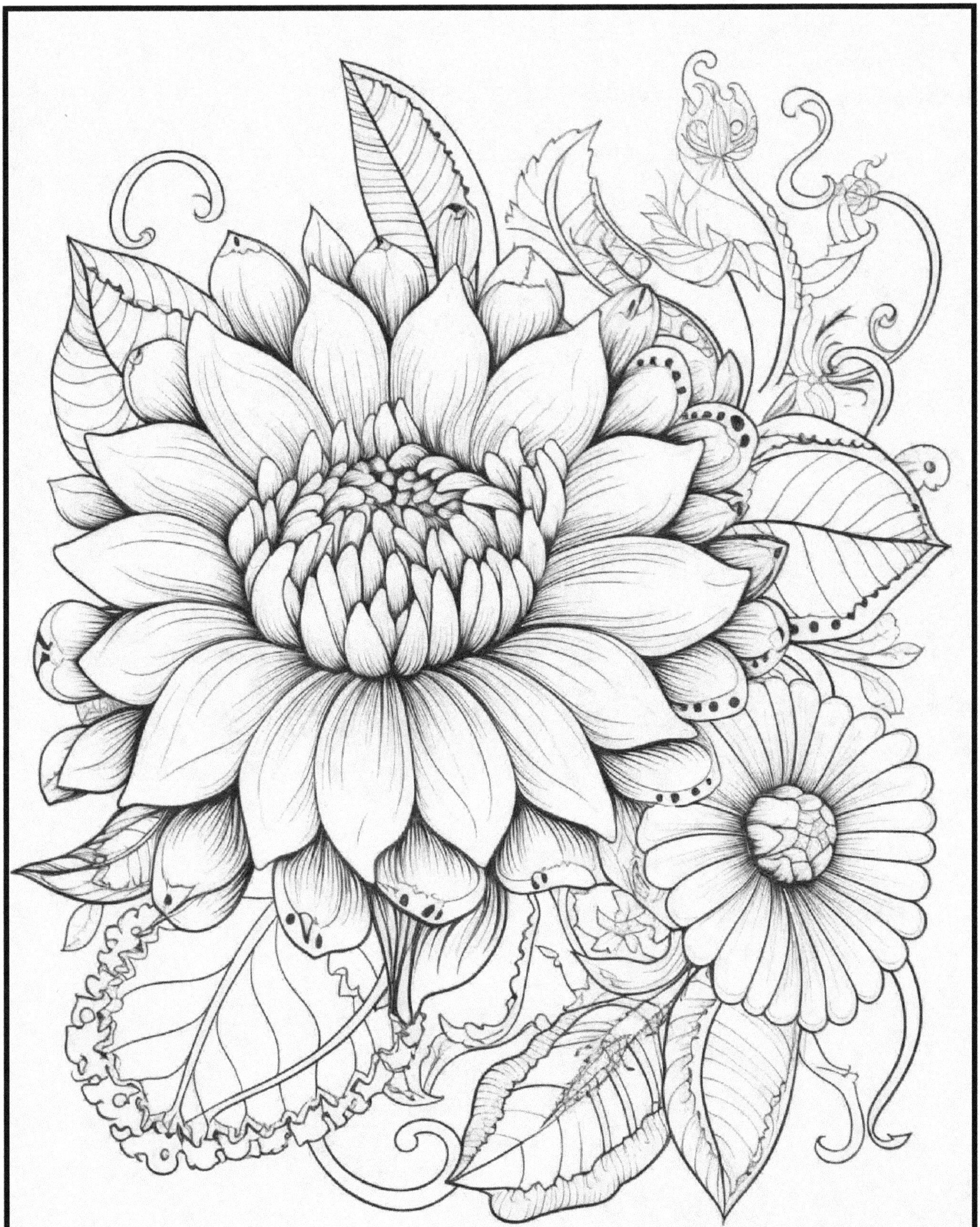

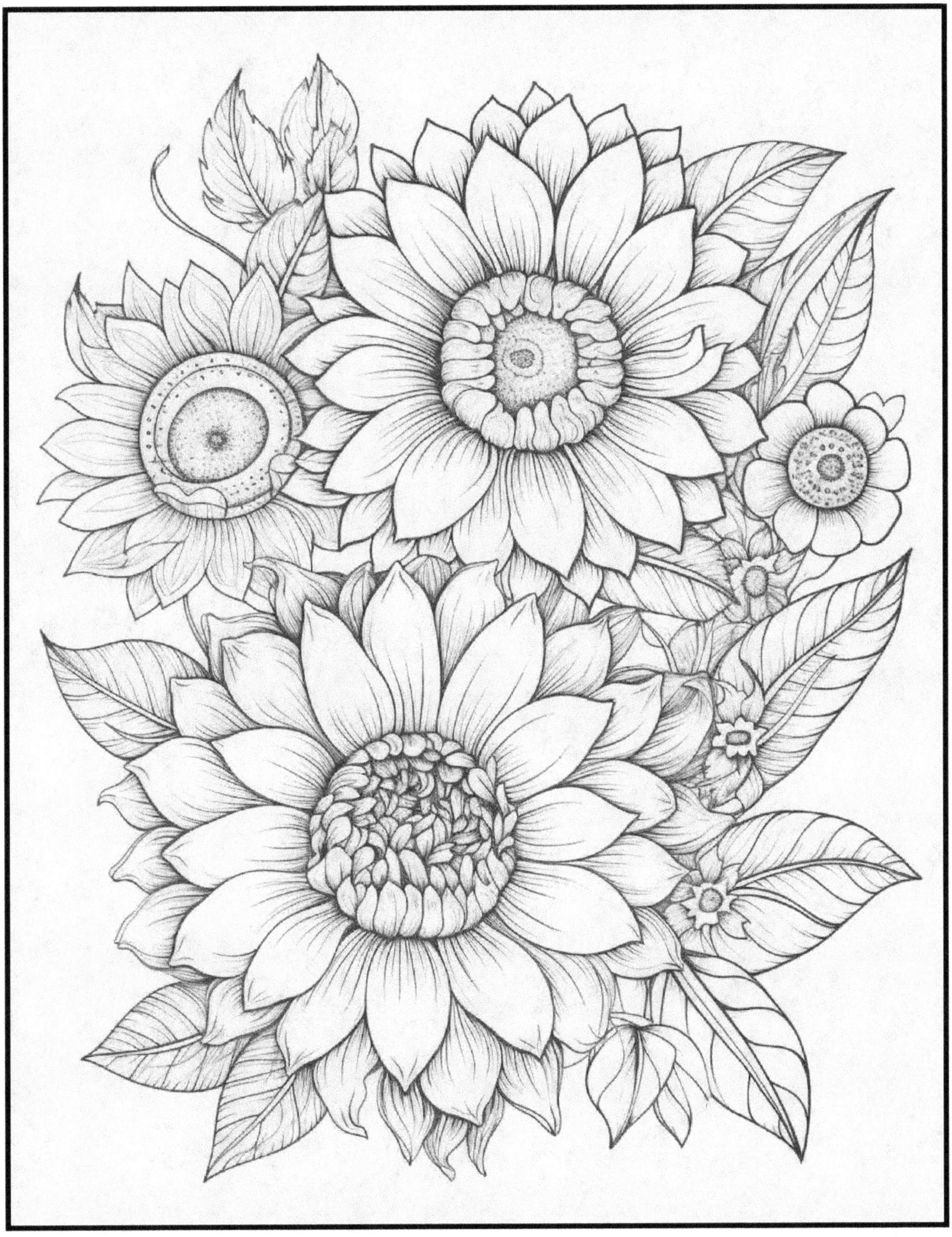

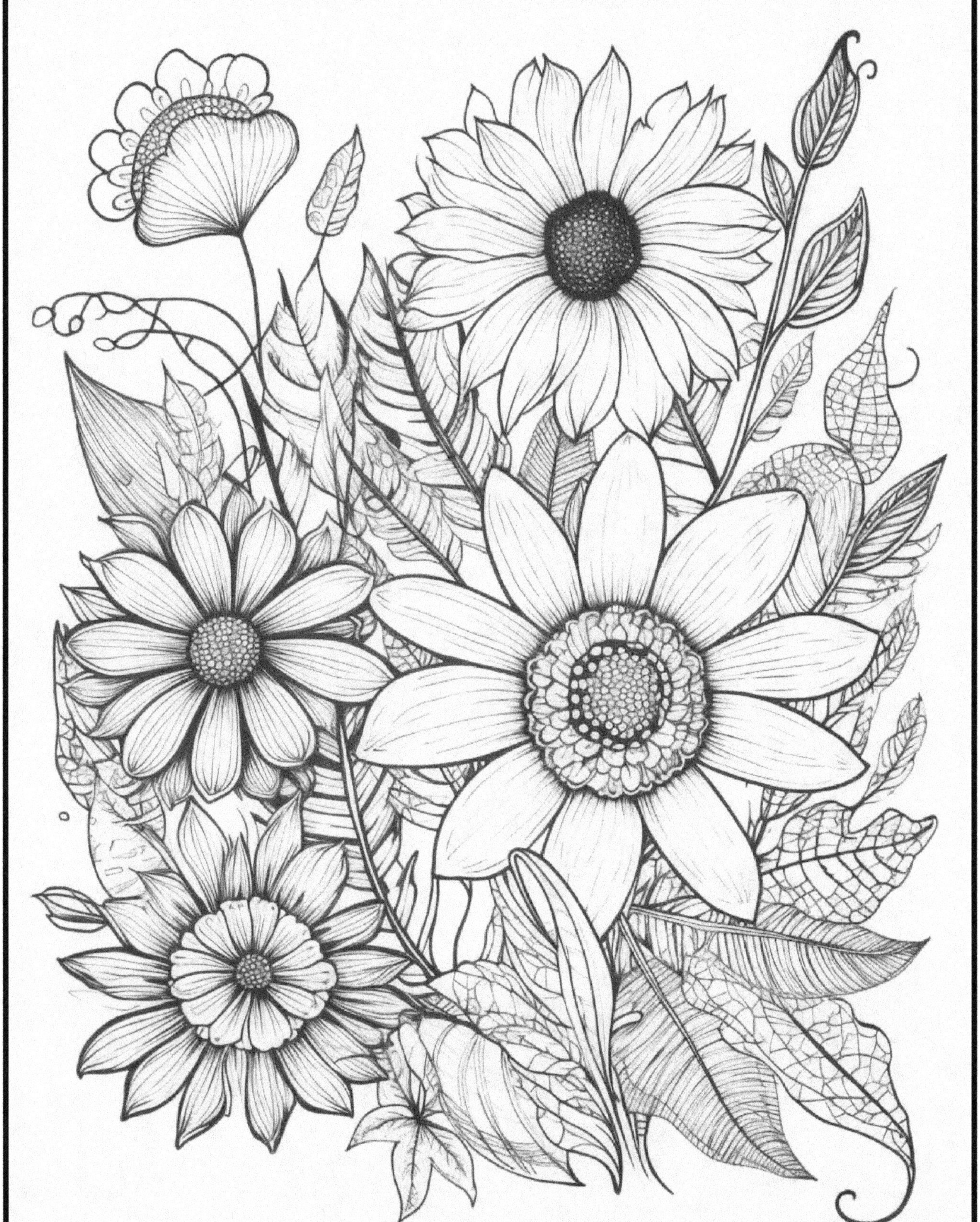

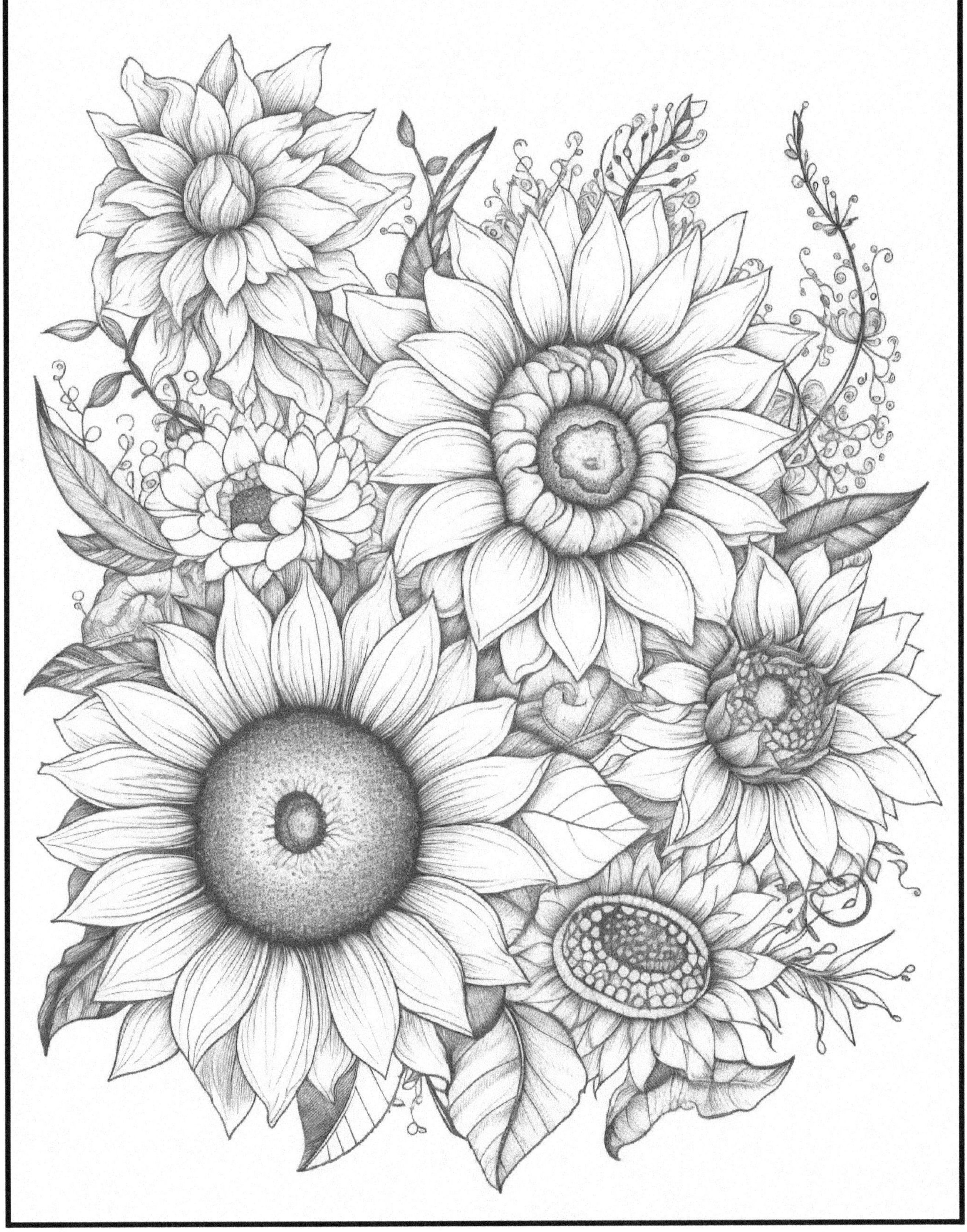

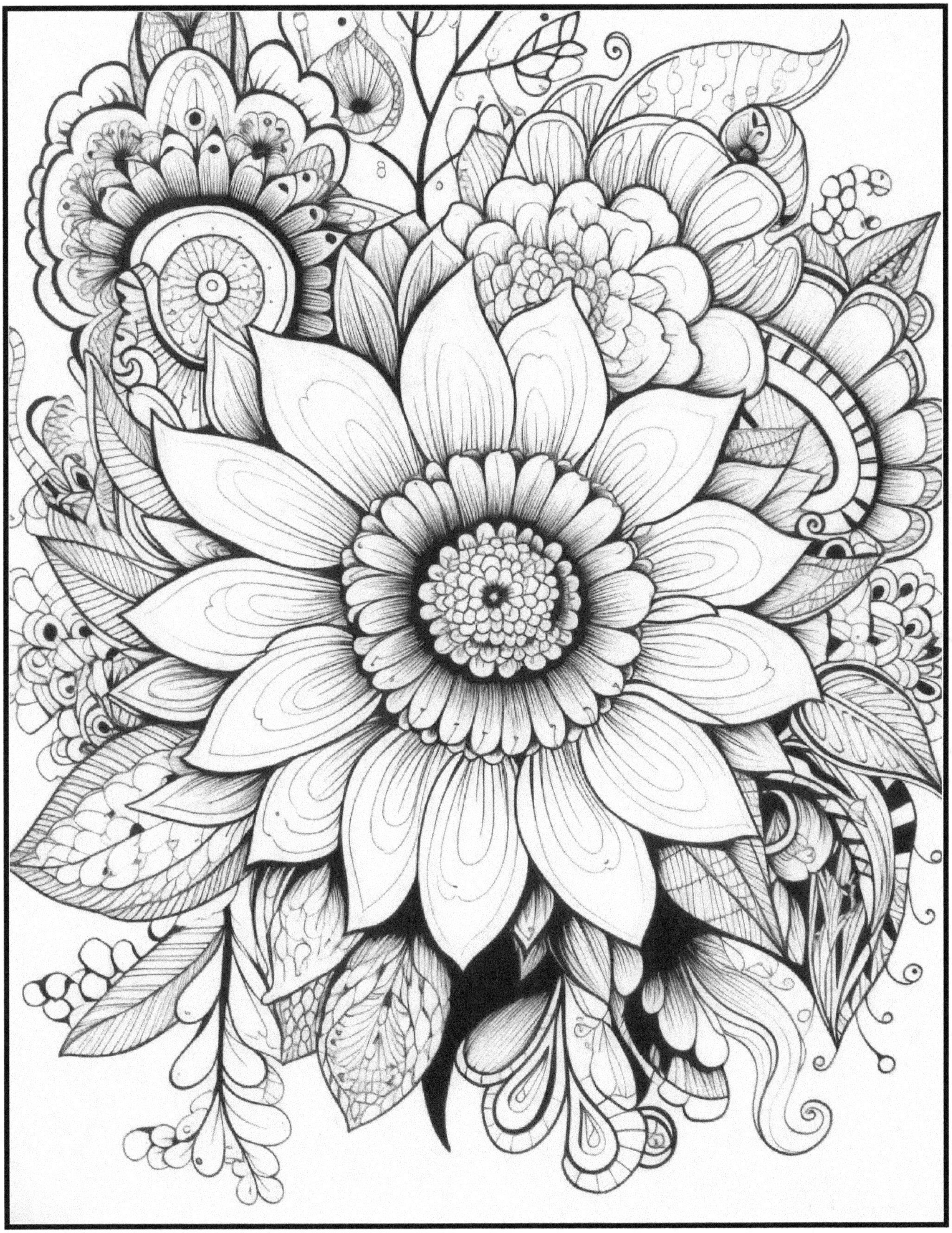

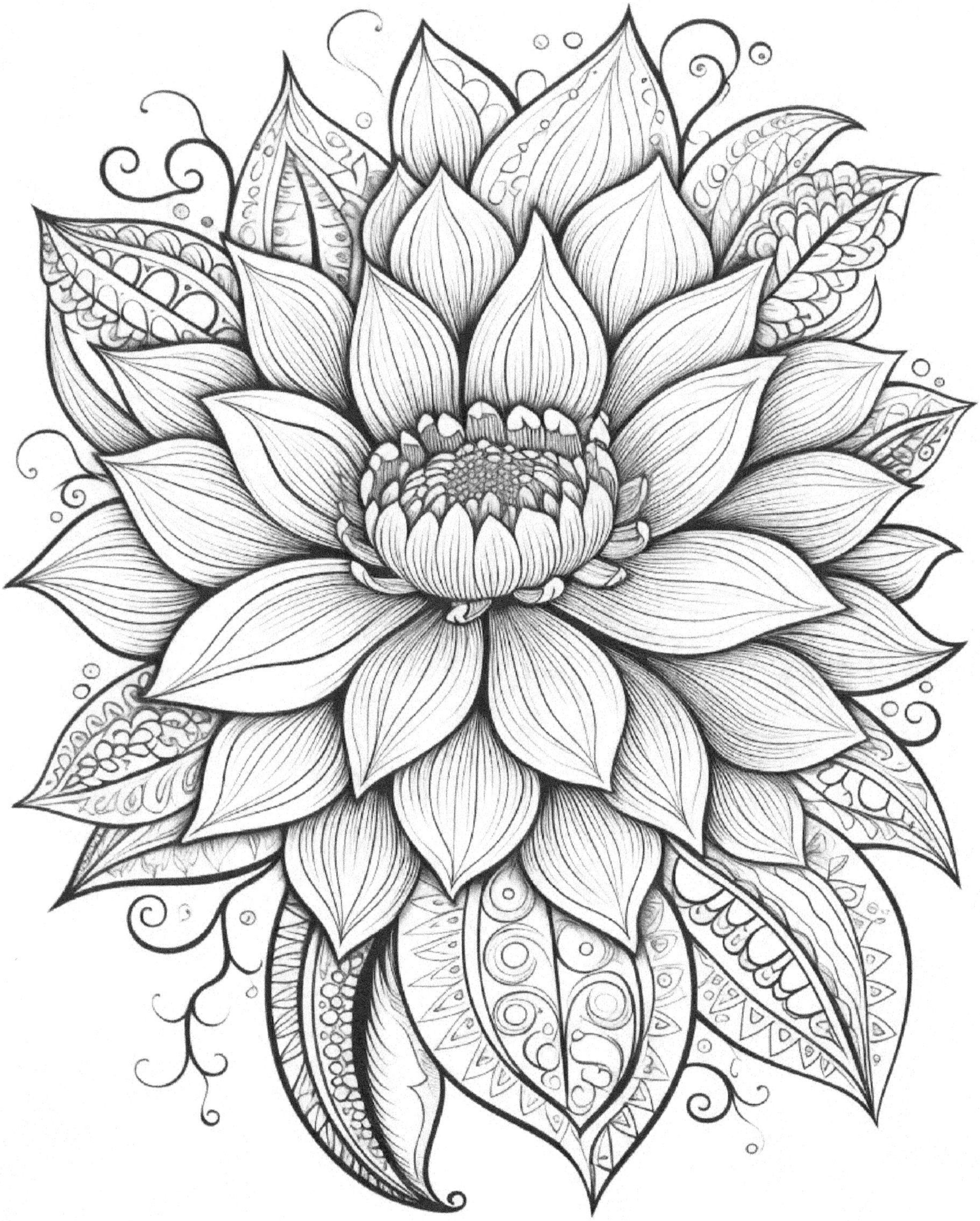

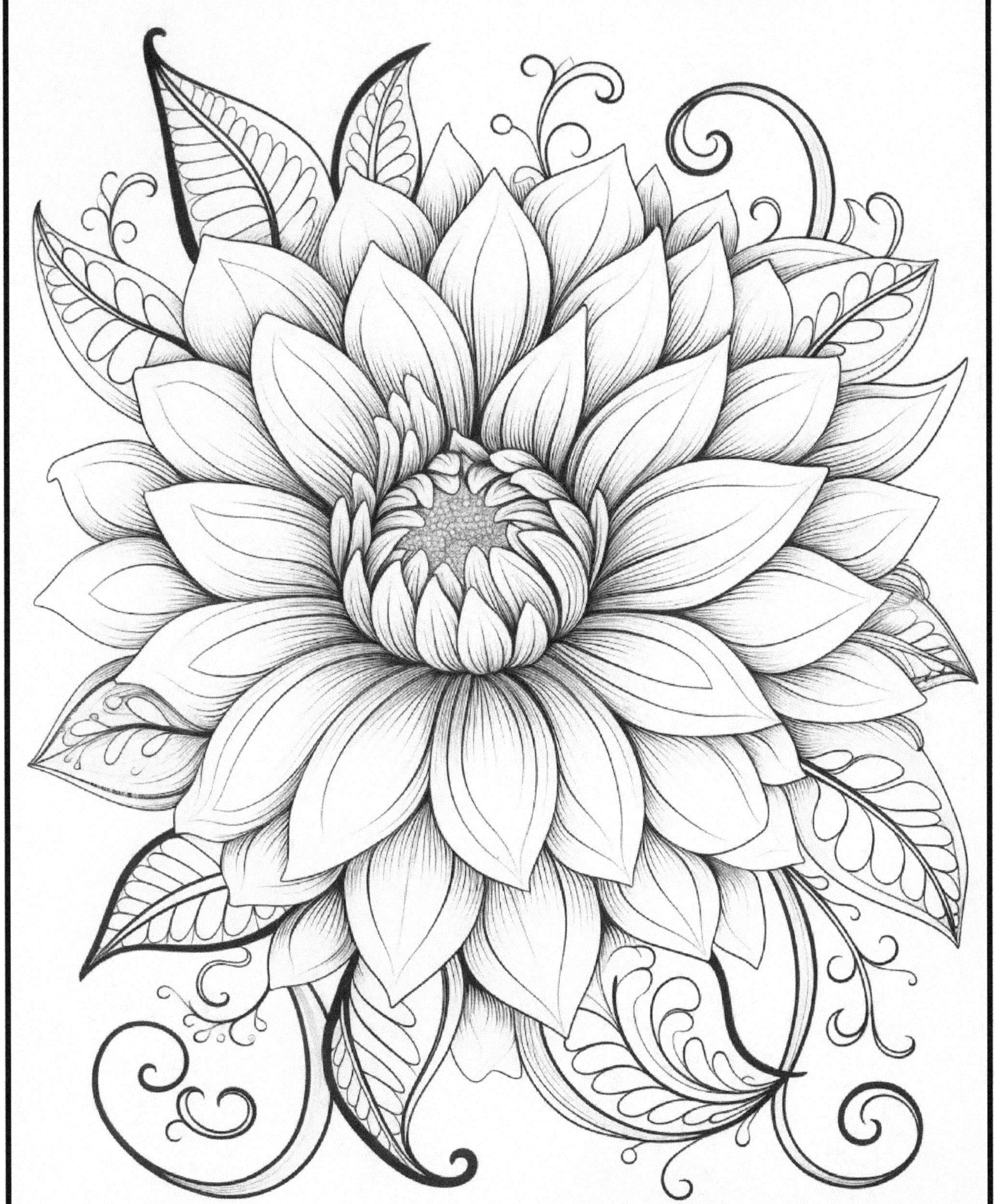

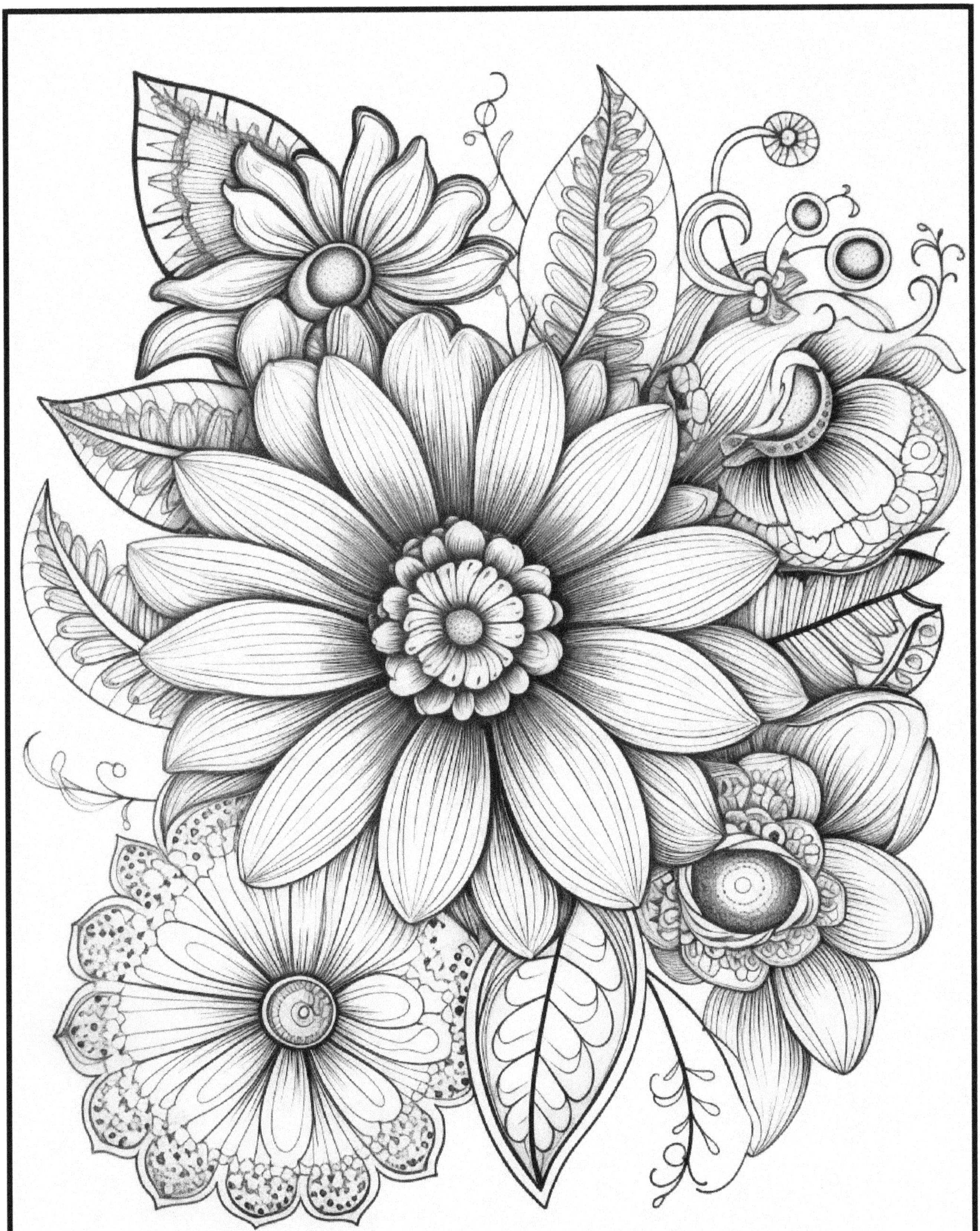

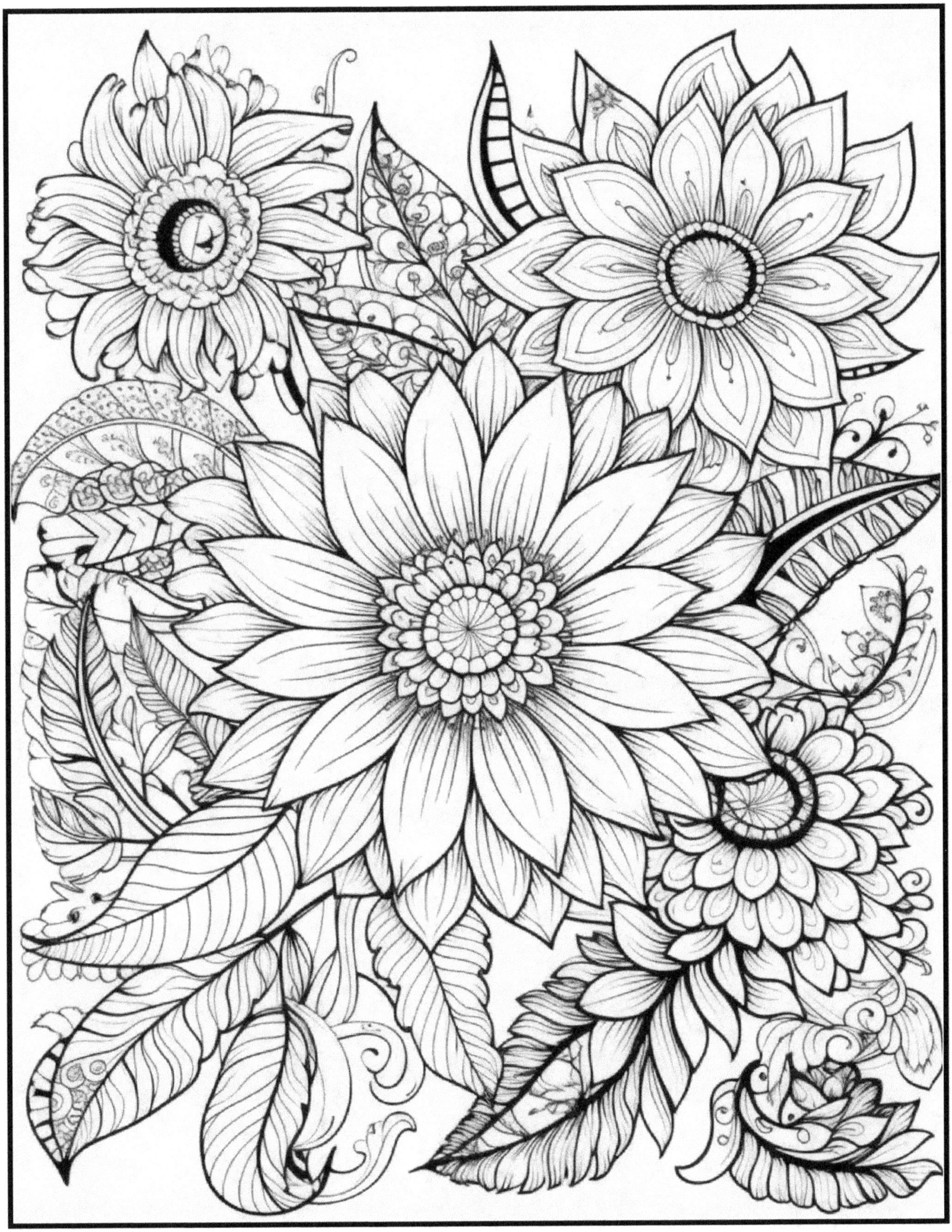

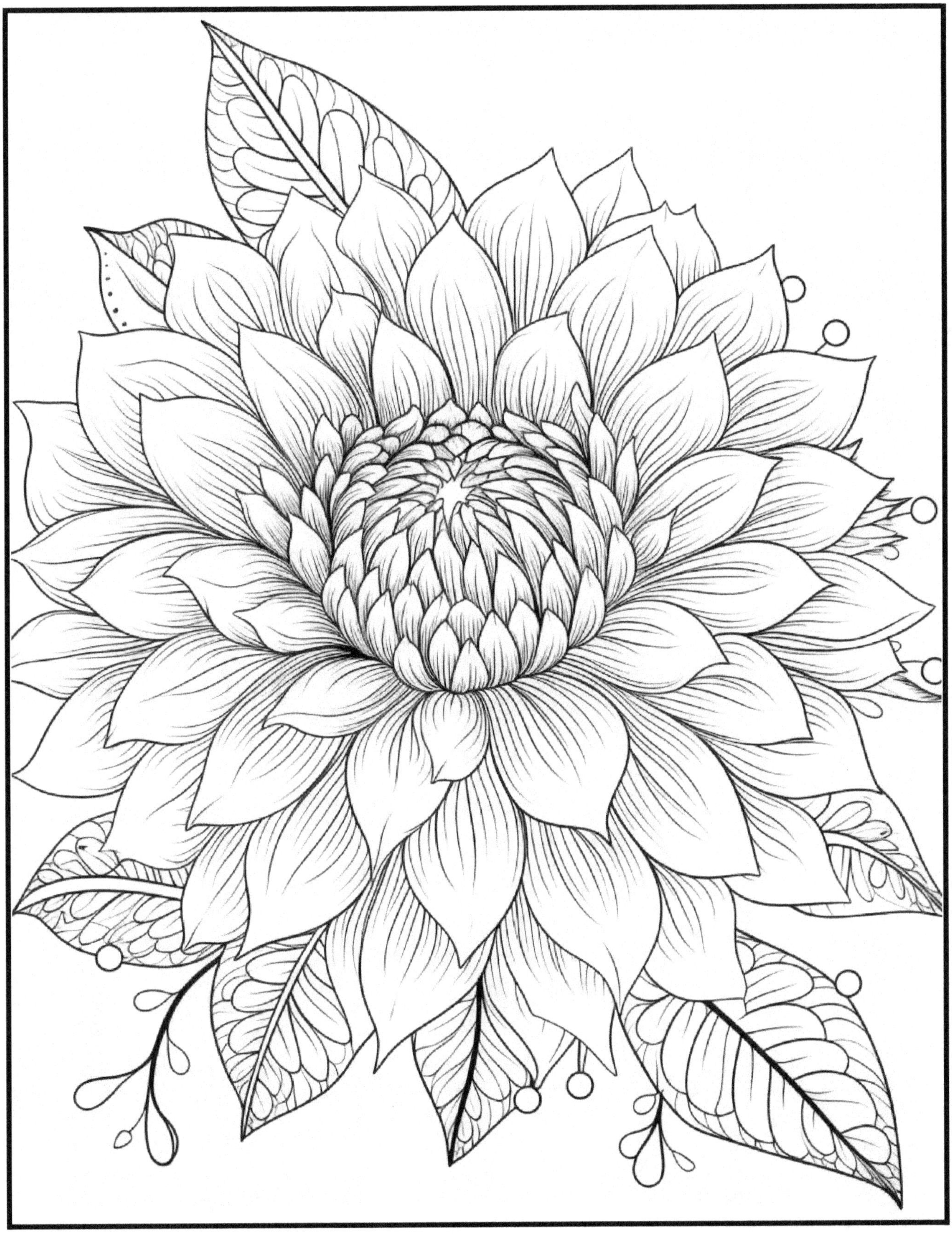

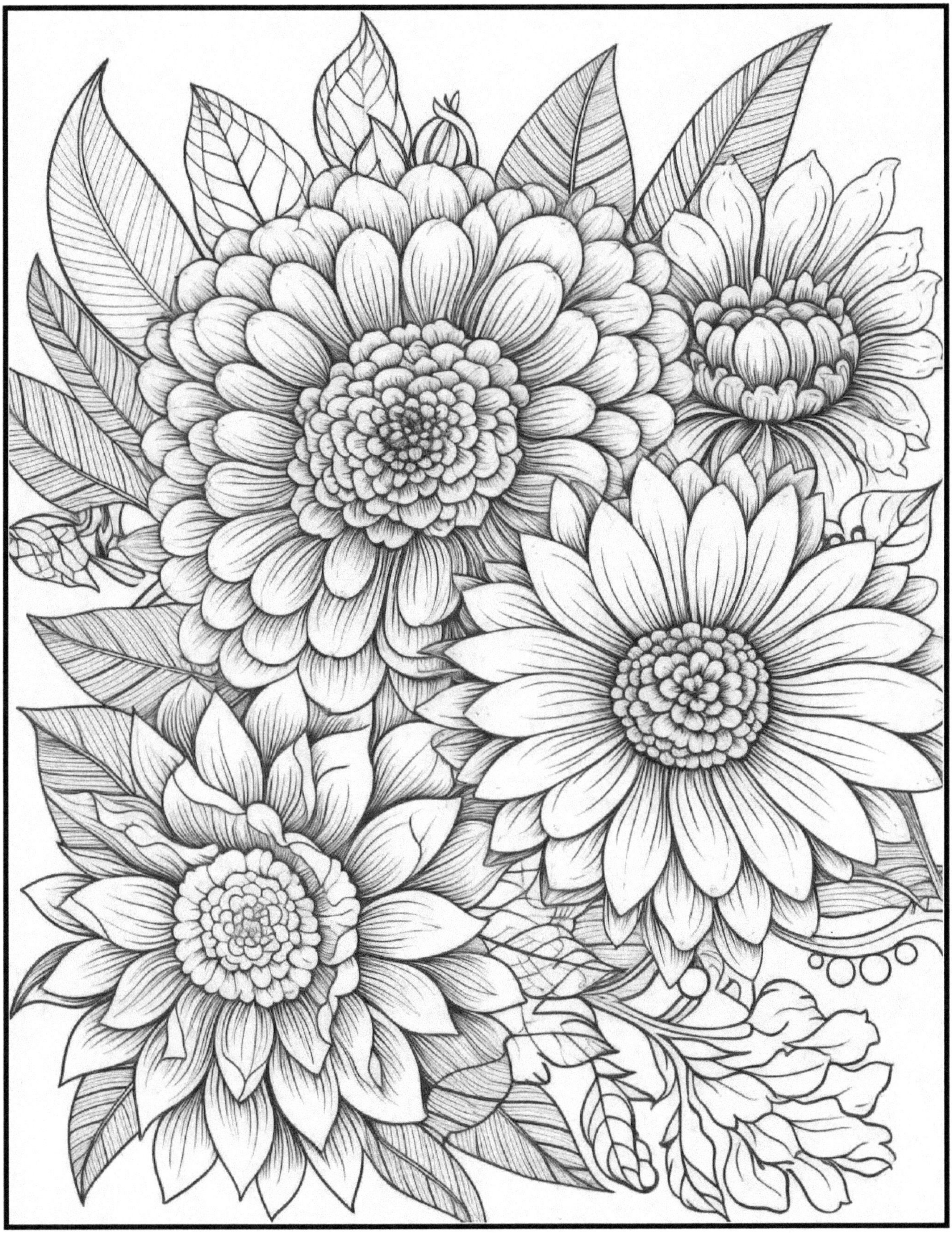

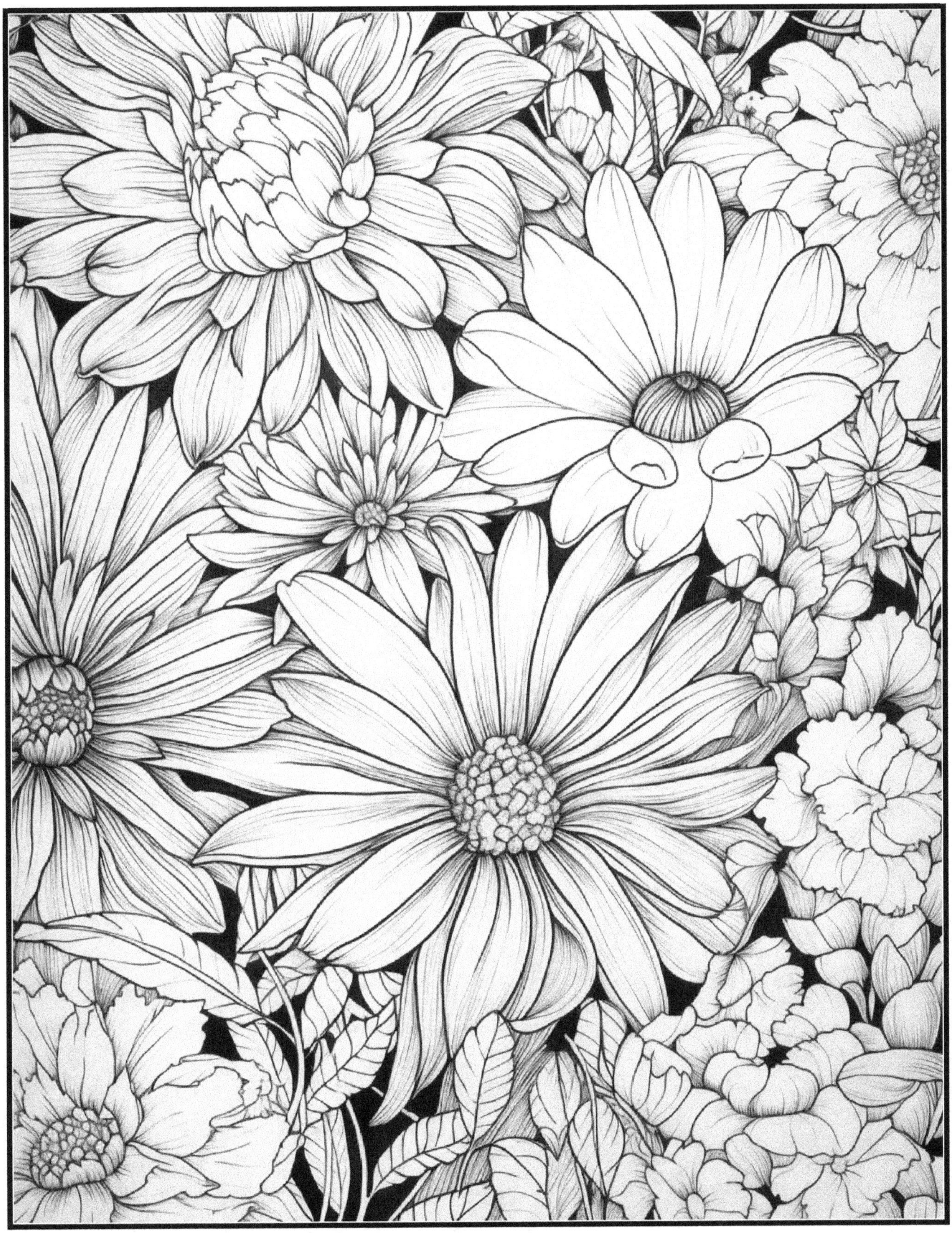

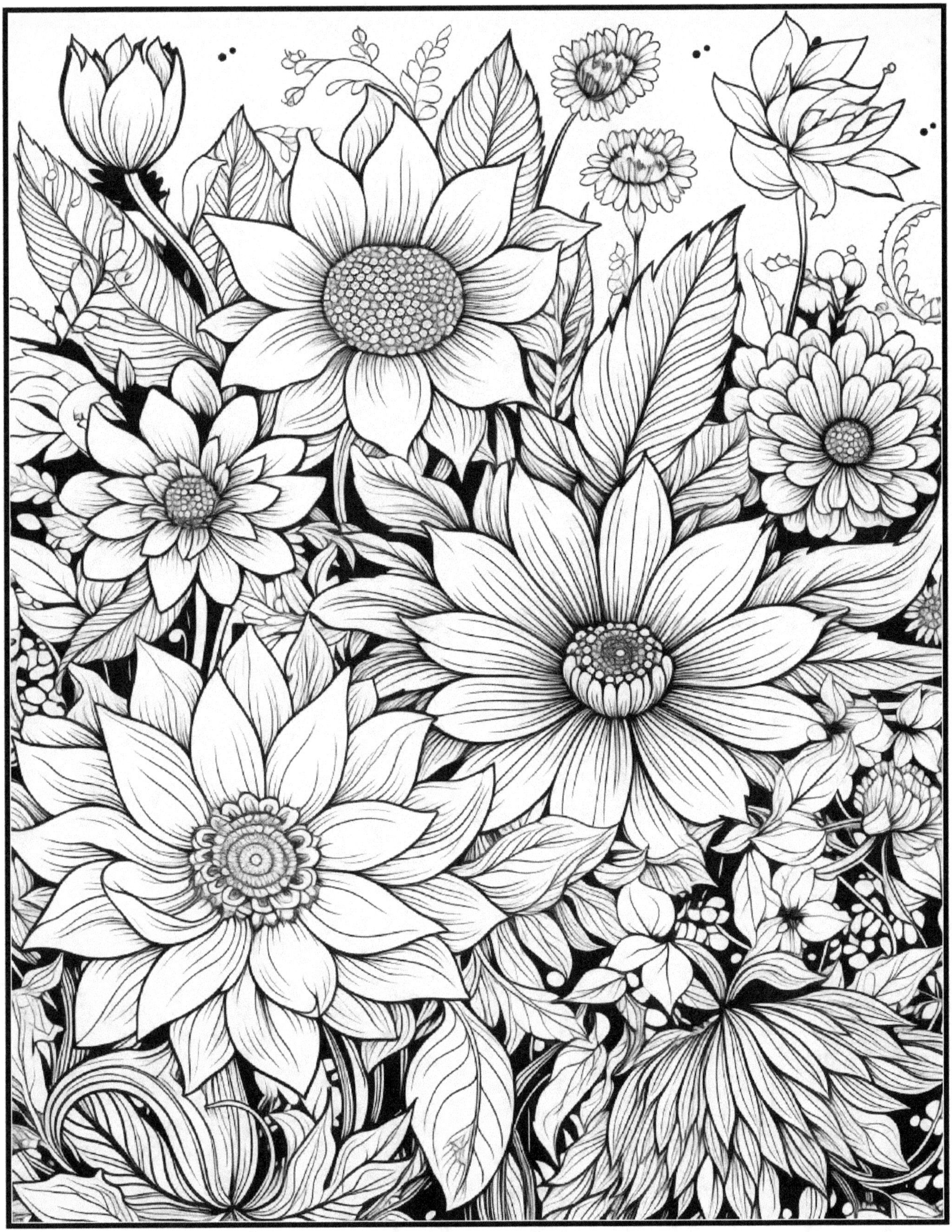

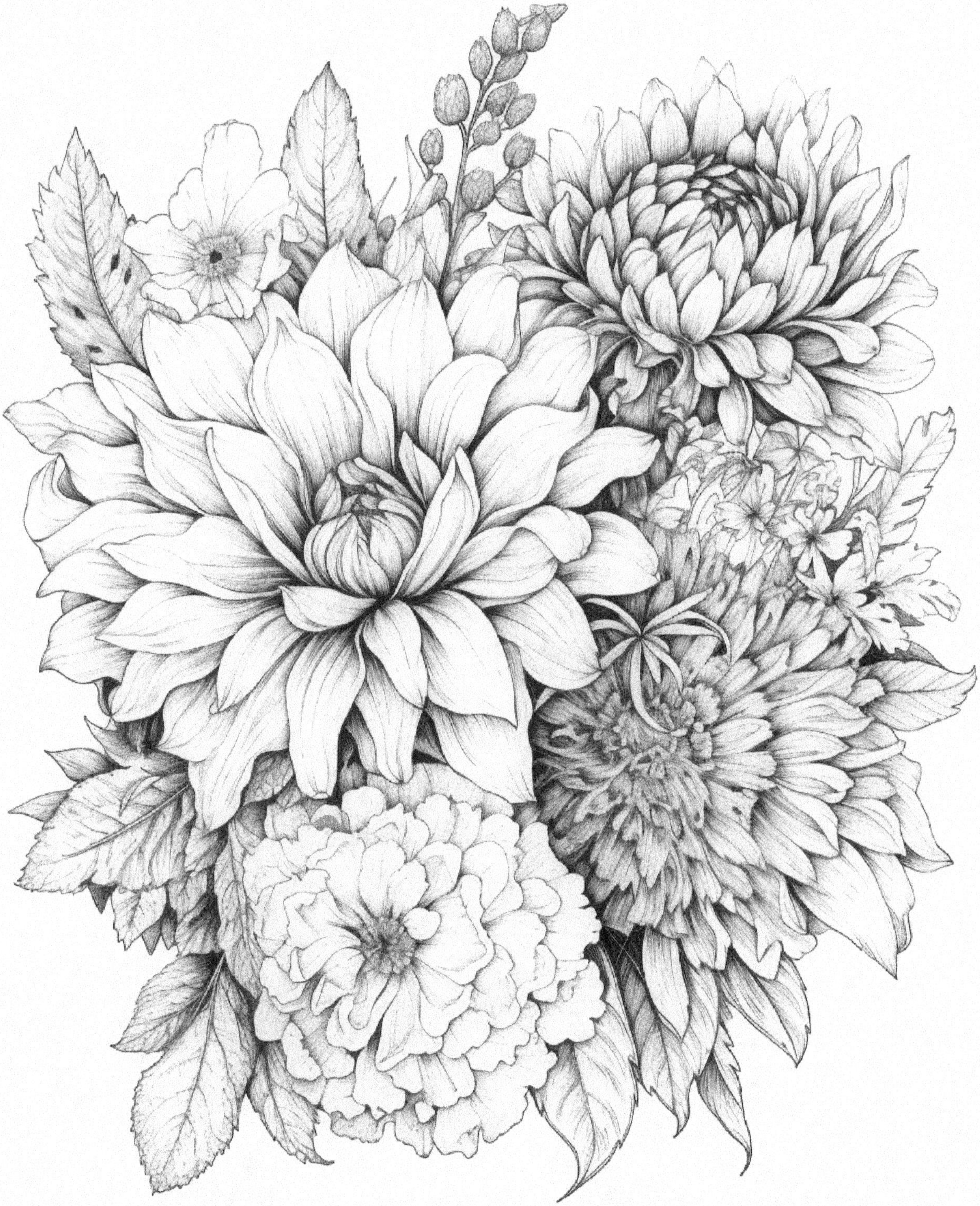

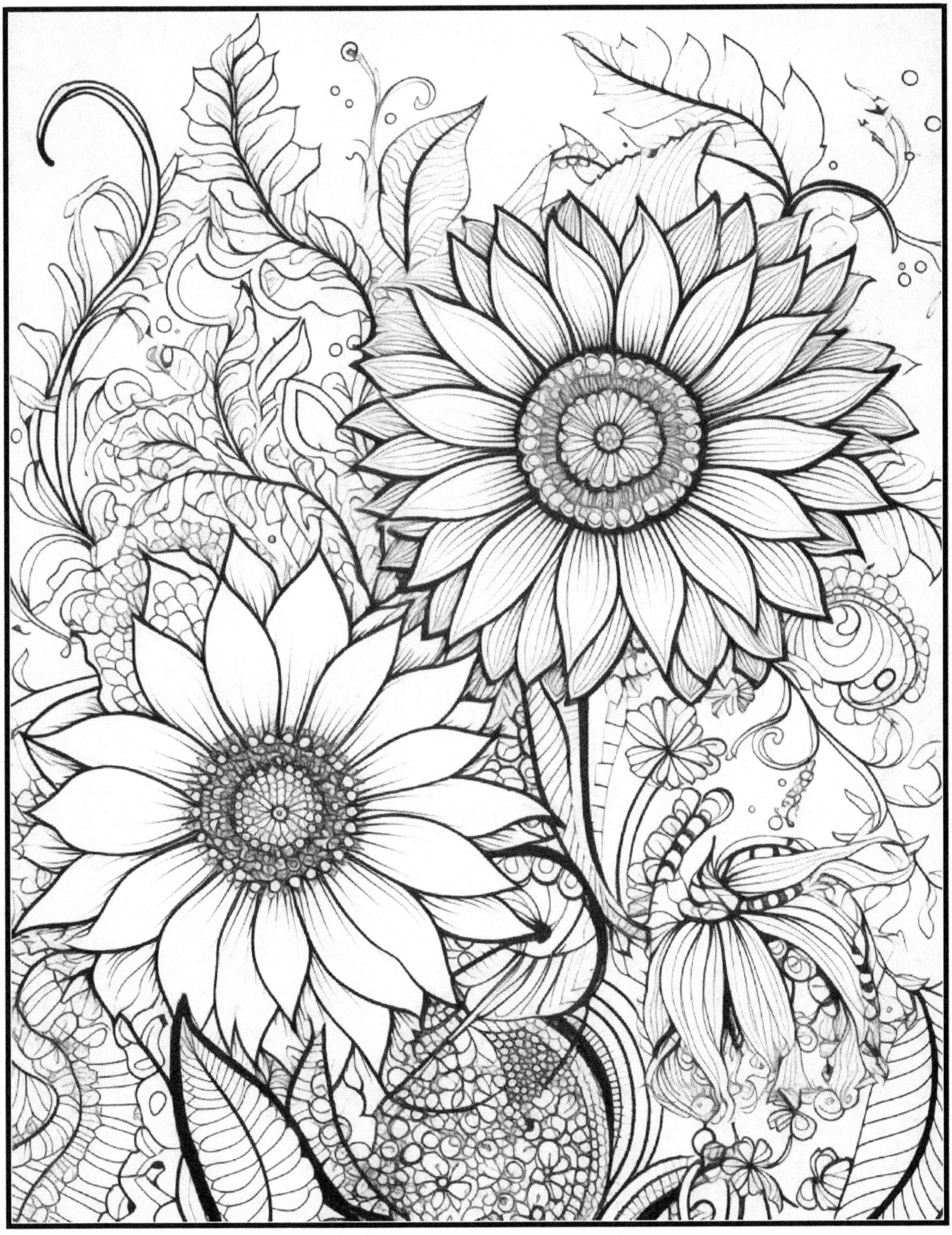

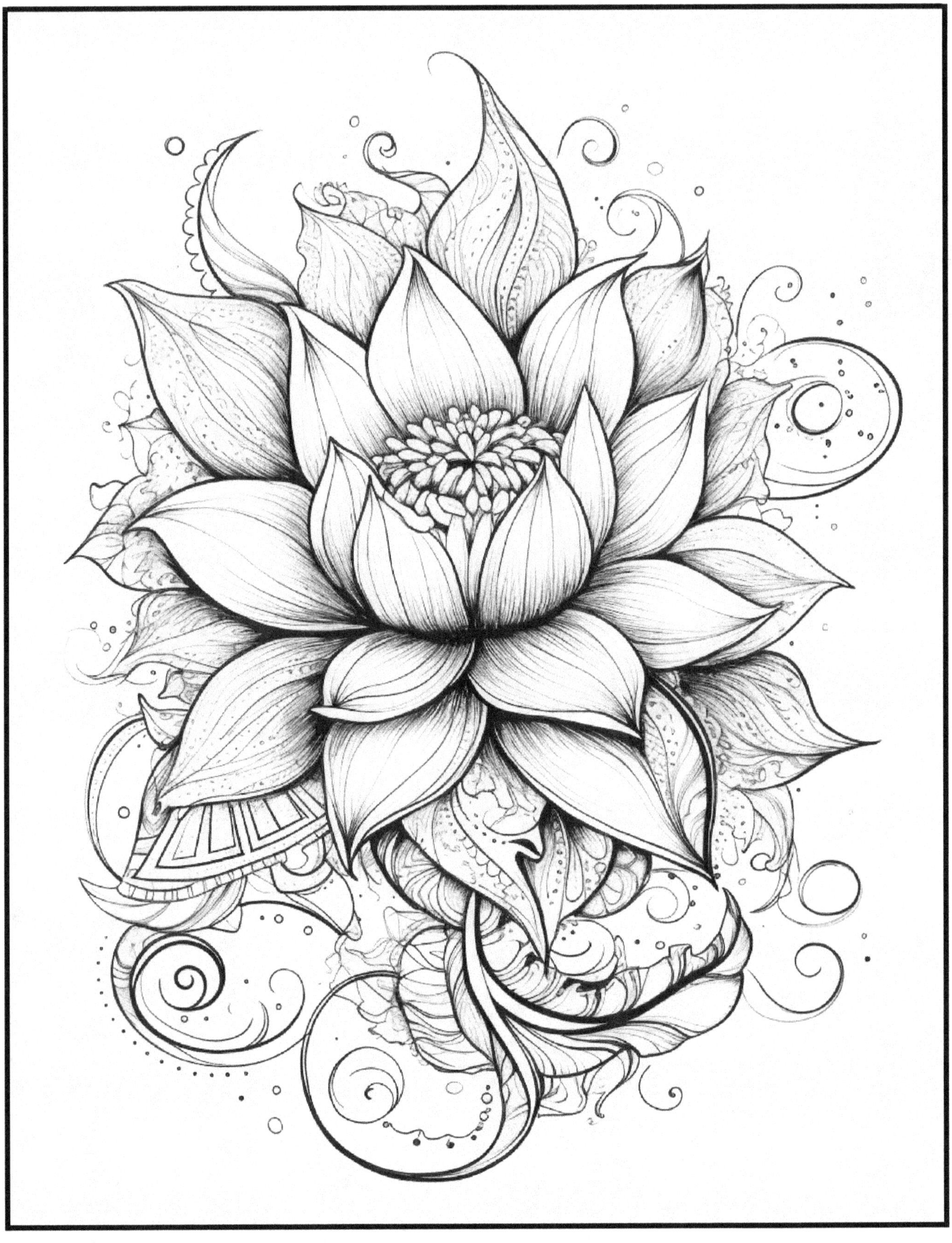

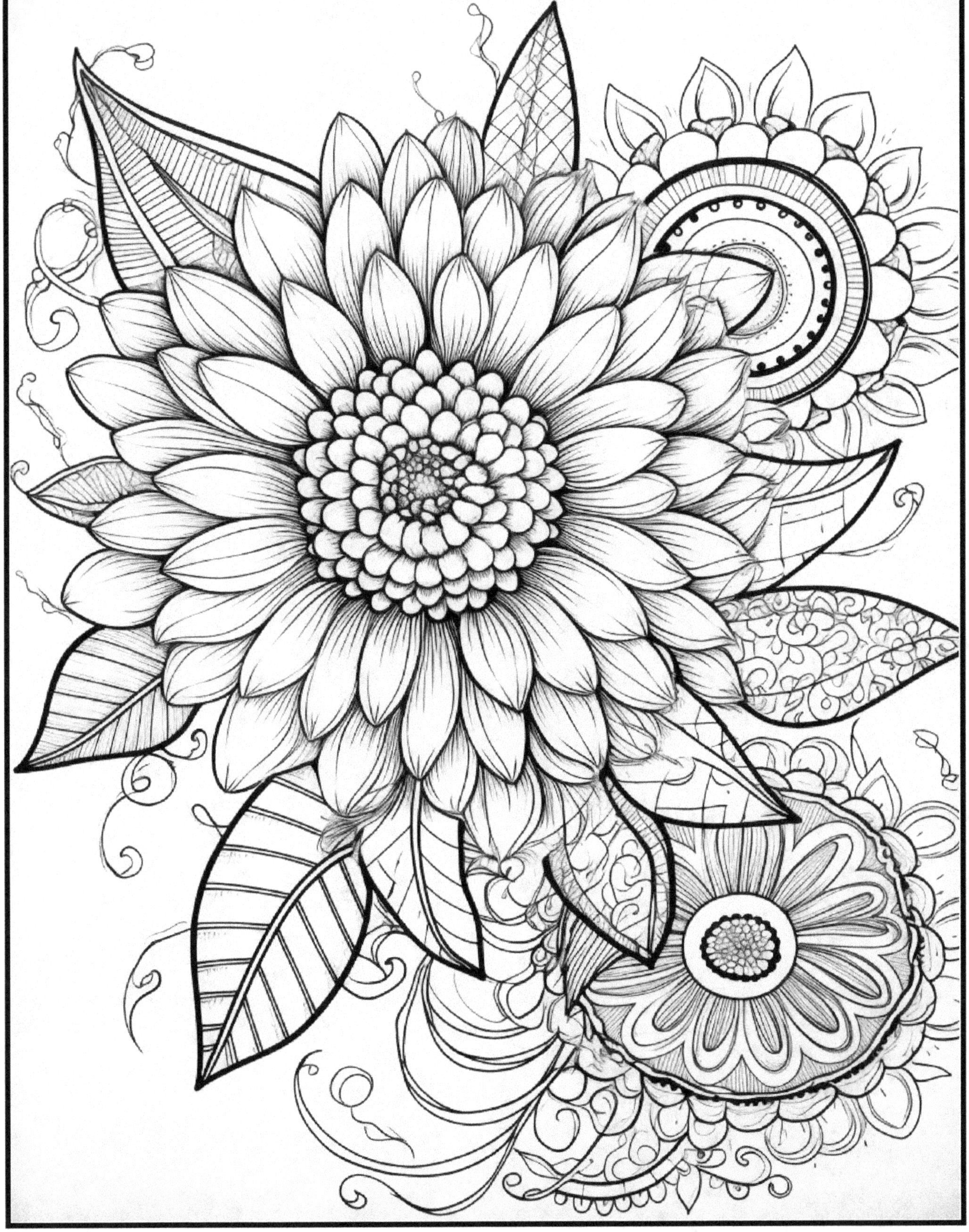

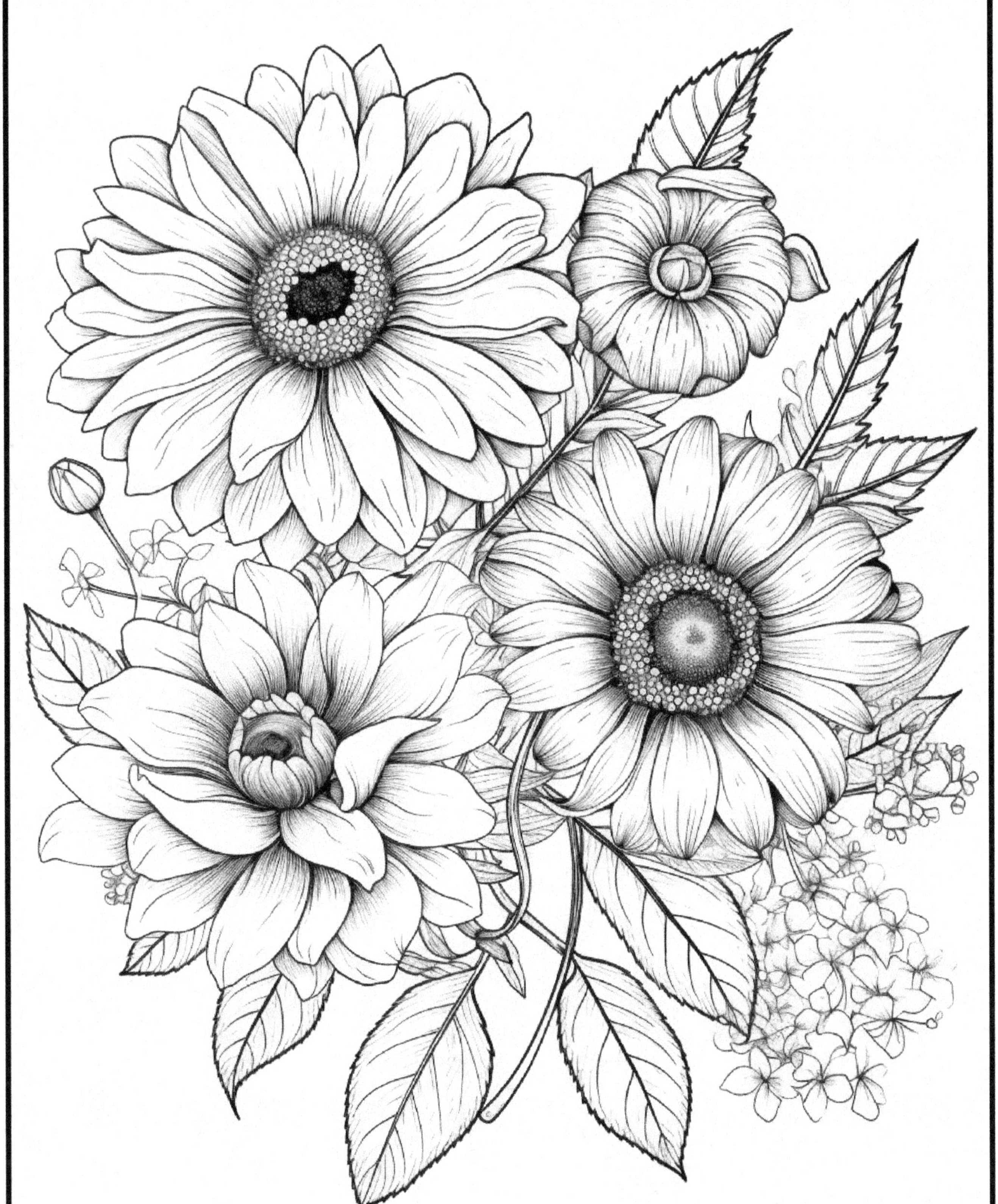

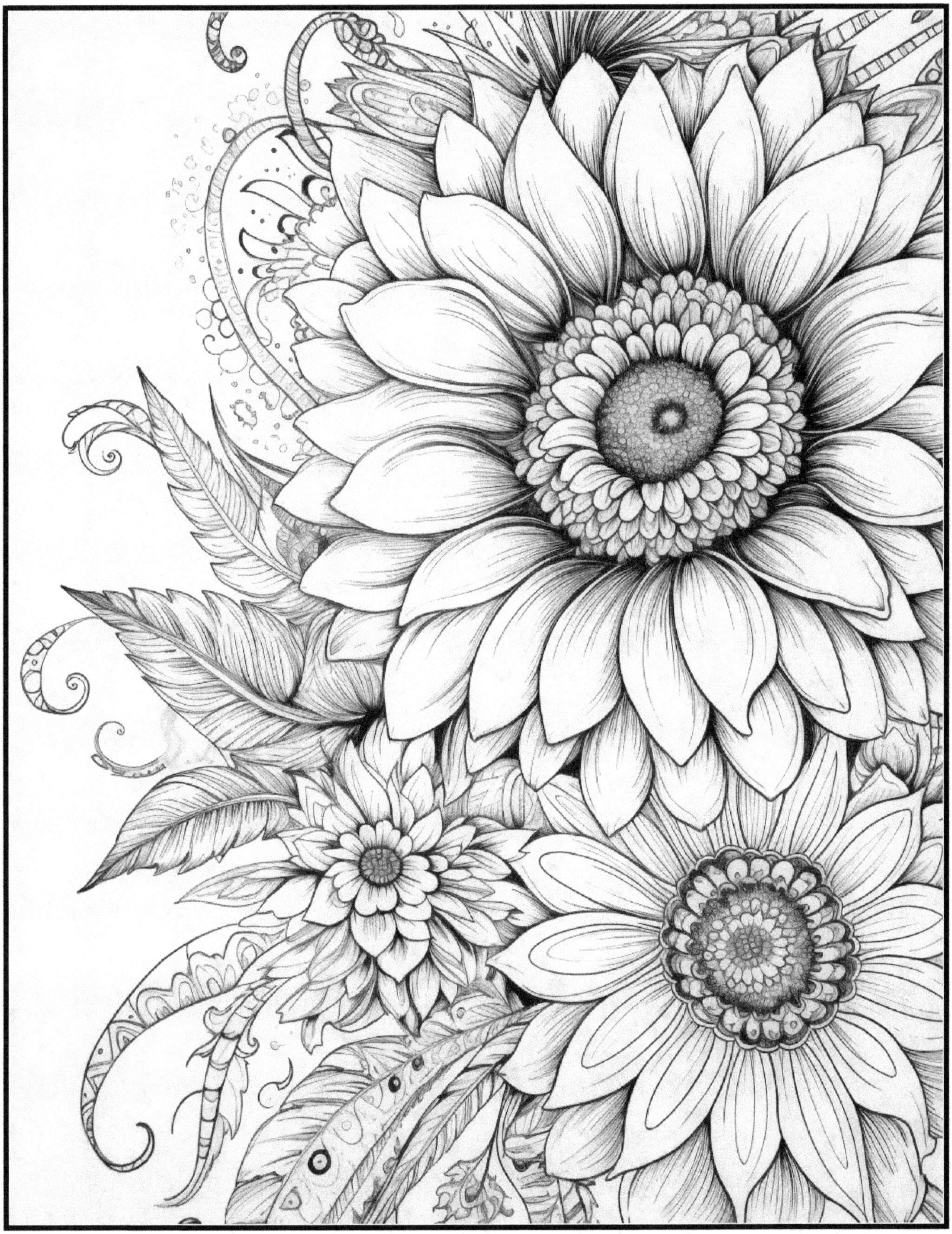

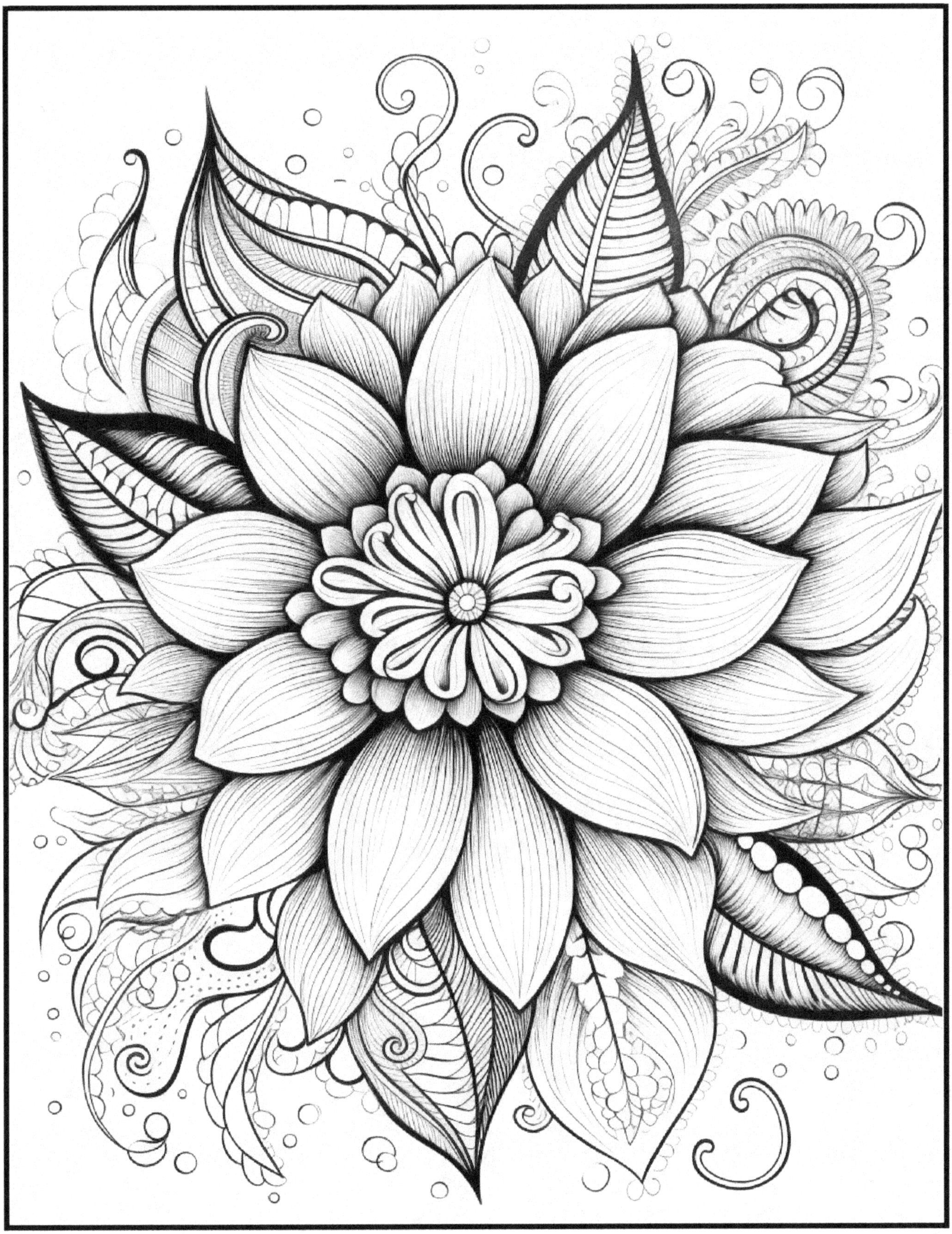

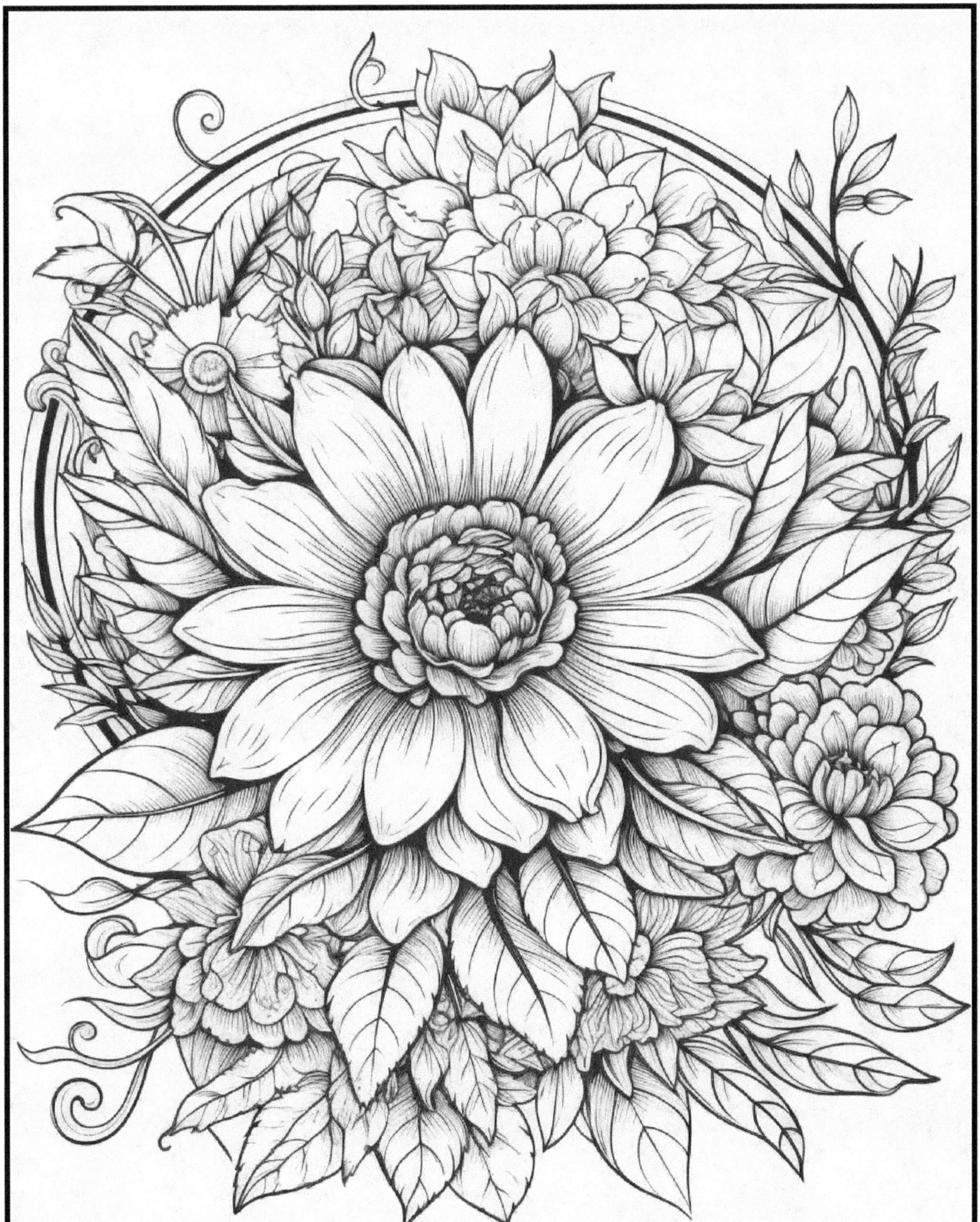

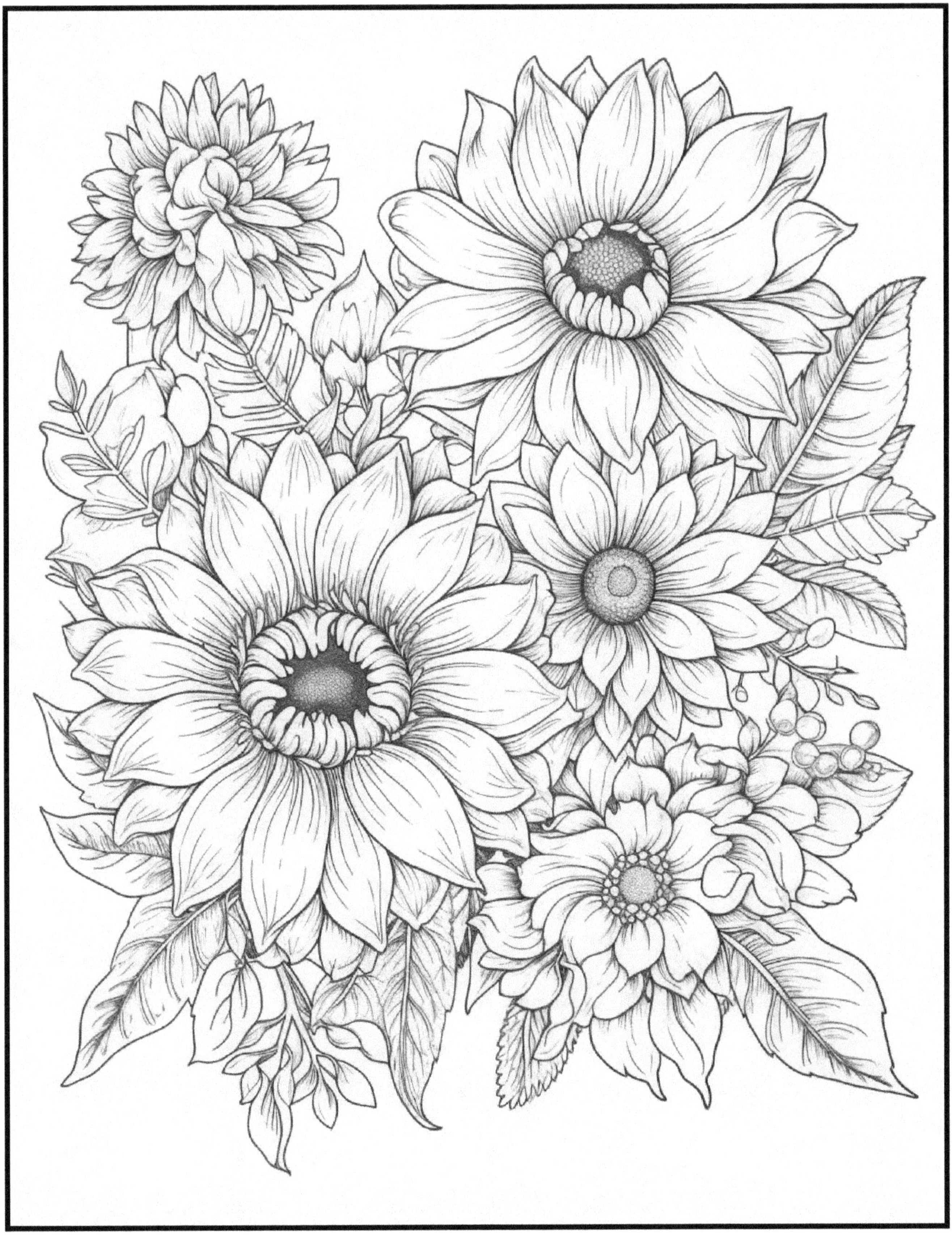

color test pages

color test pages

color test pages

color test pages

www.ingramcontent.com/pod-product-compliance
Lightning Source LLC
Chambersburg PA
CBHW080558220526
45466CB00010B/3183
* 9 7 9 8 3 9 3 6 8 5 4 3 0 *